The ULTIMATE NOAH'S ARK

Also by Mike Wilks

PILE – PETALS FROM ST KLAEDS COMPUTER
THE WEATHER WORKS
THE ULTIMATE ALPHABET
THE ANNOTATED ULTIMATE ALPHABET
THE BBC DRAWING COURSE

For Children
IN GRANNY'S GARDEN

MIKE WILKS

The ULTIMATE NOAH'S ARK

HENRY HOLT AND COMPANY
NEW YORK

For JoAnn and Alan

Henry Holt and Company, Inc.
Publishers since 1866
115 West 18th Street
New York, New York 10011

Henry Holt® is a registered trademark of
Henry Holt and Company, Inc.

First published in the United States in 1993
by Henry Holt and Company, Inc.
Published in Canada by Fitzhenry & Whiteside Ltd.,
91 Granton Drive, Richmond Hill, Ontario L4B 2N5.
Originally published in Great Britain in 1993
by Michael Joseph Ltd., part of the Penguin Group.

Library of Congress Cataloging-in-Publication Data
Wilks, Mike.
The ultimate Noah's ark / Mike Wilks. — 1st American ed.
p.   cm.
I. Wilks, Mike.   2. Noah's ark in art.   I. Title.
ND497.W638A4 93–4021 CIP
759.2 — dc20
ISBN 0-8050-2802-1

Henry Holt books are available for special promotions and
premiums. For details contact: Director, Special Markets.

First American Edition — 1993

Printed in Italy
All first editions are printed on acid-free paper.∞

1   3   5   7   9   10   8   6   4   2

ACKNOWLEDGMENT
The author and publishers would like to thank the Department of Zoology at
The Natural History Museum, London, for their invaluable help in checking and verifying the text.

PICTURE CREDITS
page 6   "The Arrangement of the Ark" from *Arca Noë*. The British Library, London.

page 7   "Noah's Ark" by Edward Hicks. Philadelphia Museum of Art: Bequest of Lisa Norris Elkins.

page 8   "The Animals Entering The Ark" by Bartolo di Fredi.
Collegiata, S. Gimignano/Bridgeman Art Library, London.

page 9   "The Animals Going into The Ark" by Jacopo Bassano.
Prado, Madrid/Bridgeman Art Library, London.

INTRODUCTION

How is it possible to look at something without seeing it? It happens all the time and, even though I am acutely aware of the way the eyes slide off things without noticing them, I am not immune from it and often have to make a conscious effort to use my eyes in that special way known as *seeing*. This is what this book is all about. Just as I used this most highly developed of the human senses in creating this book so you too must use your sense of sight to solve the mystery that I am about to set before you. But before we begin we need to start at the beginning – the very beginning.

Once upon a time there was no time. There was nothing. Neither time nor space, life nor death, sound nor colour, matter nor consciousness: just unimaginable nothingness. Then, in an incomprehensibly violent instant, eternity began and *everything* was created. Immediately after this Big Bang, 'everything' was in the form of elemental particles that gradually cooled and formed into atoms which, in turn, coalesced into clouds of primeval gas and, ultimately, into stars. These lived out their awesomely long lives and died and were reborn. As the universe continued to cool and expand, these newborn stars formed innumerable galaxies separated from each other by the inexpressible vastness of cold, empty space. Each galaxy contained countless stars and, gradually, the amorphous matter around at least one of these stars collapsed in on itself to form planets. Agonizingly slowly, primitive, self-replicating life evolved on one of these planets and, as the aeons crept by, these insidious specks of life began to tame the atmosphere and prepare the way for more complex life forms. The atmosphere gradually changed and Earth calmed. As life continued its ponderous evolution it adapted and diversified, first in the seas and later emerging on to the land, until mankind eventually evolved as a separate species.

One moment, ages later, man's consciousness crossed a kind of threshold and he chose to differentiate himself from the rest of the natural world. From that point on his relationship with the other creatures with which he shares this planet began to become complicated. He recognized that he was an animal himself yet, in some ineffable way, different: a paradox that remains unresolved to this day. We think of animals as base and primitive, but we admire them for the very qualities that we have discarded. We name our automobiles, war machines and sporting teams after them in the hope of taking on these essential 'animal' qualities. Each nation has its own emblematic creature and the universe is studded with constellations bearing animal names.

Animals also feature throughout history in the world's religions in a variety of rôles. Almost the entire ancient Egyptian pantheon comprised zoomorphic gods and goddesses and several of the Hindu god Vishnu's traditional ten avatars, or incarnations, are in animal form. This numinous quality conveyed by animals is also present in Christianity where the Evangelists Mark, Luke and John are symbolized respectively as a lion, a bull and an eagle. Anyone who has even a passing acquaintance with the Bible will recognize the symbolic meanings attached to, say, the serpent, the lamb and the dove.

One of the most evocative and powerful Bible stories is that of Noah and his Ark. In the legend God commands Noah to collect a male and female of every living creature – 'two and two of all flesh, wherein is the breath of life' – and to build an Ark to save them from the flood that He is about to send to destroy a corrupt world. God even specified the material (gopher wood) and the dimensions of the Ark as 300 cubits long, 50 cubits wide and 30 cubits high. A cubit was the distance from the elbow to the tip of the extended middle finger – about 45cm (nearly 18in) for an adult – which gives a size of about $135 \times 22.5 \times 13.5$m (approximately $443 \times 74 \times 44$ft). Even the doors, windows and numbers of storeys (three) were specified. Seldom are legends this exact. God then caused it to rain for forty days and forty nights, destroying all life on the Earth except for that safely ensconced in the Ark. After the flood abated Noah released all of the creatures and they, and his family, subsequently increased and repopulated the world.

Interestingly, the story of a great flood and the near destruction of mankind occurs in many religions throughout the world. A myth of the people of the Lower Congo recounts how the moon met the sun, making it lose its brilliance and

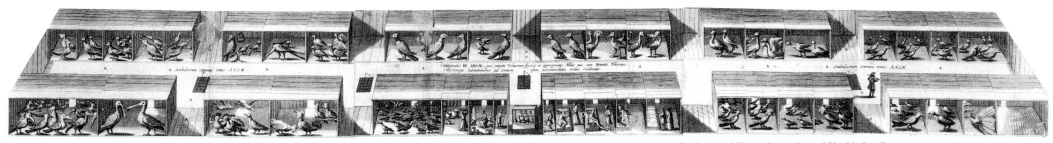

'The Arrangement of the Ark' from *Arca Noë*, published 1673. This detail depicts the upper storey of the Ark with peafowl, spoonbills, owls, storks and Noah's family

caused a flood. The men were then changed into monkeys and the women into lizards after which modern man was created. There are several Inca legends of a flood, one of which tells how the few survivors took refuge on the summit of a floating mountain. A similar tale comes from Samoa where the survivors of the deluge were rescued by the god Tangaloa, who commanded his servants to raise the Samoan archipelago from the waters as a refuge. The Hindu *Satapatha Brahmana* tells how Manu – the first man (and from whose name the English word 'man' is partly derived) – caught a rainbow-coloured fish that he subsequently released into the sea. In return for this kindness the fish warned Manu of the coming deluge and told him to load a giant boat with two of every species of animal and the seeds of every plant. The flood came drowning everything but the boat and its occupants and the fish, now grown to enormous size, reappeared and towed it to safety on a mountaintop. Manu's saviour turned out to be Matsyavatara, the god Vishnu's fish avatar.

In fact, the Bible story has an almost identical counterpart in the Assyro-Babylonian 'Epic of Creation' and it would seem reasonable to assume that they share the same origin. For unexplained reasons, Bel and the other gods decided to drown the world, but the god Ea was overheard confiding the plan by an inhabitant of Shuruppak, named Uta-Napishtim, on the banks of the Euphrates. He then built a vessel not unlike the Ark, though the dimensions were reportedly somewhat greater as the height was 120 cubits. Besides his family and the animals, 'the seeds of all life', he prudently took aboard all his gold and silver. The deluge lasted seven days and seven nights after which all living creatures, with the exception of those aboard the vessel, were changed into mud. The two stories are so close that Uta-Napishtim even sends out a swallow, a raven and a dove to search for dry land but, unlike Noah's birds, none of them returns.

Like all great stories, the legend of Noah's Ark can be read on a number of levels. One can simply read it as a colourful and amusing fable or as a Christian parable in which the soul is borne through the trials and tribulations of earthly existence by the ark of faith. Some even view it as a historical account of the drowning of the continent of Atlantis, described by Plato in his dialogues, the *Timaeus* and the *Critias*. It also assumes a deeper significance common to all myths where the Ark becomes the human psyche wherein balance and harmony must be achieved for the fractured individual to become whole once more. The inclusion of the male and female creatures in the vessel of the ark can be seen as echoing the 'chymical wedding' of European alchemy with the marriage of the male and female elements of the sun and moon, gold and silver, within the one body, thus turning the base 'Materia Prima' of matter into the 'Lapis Philosophorum', or philosopher's stone, of the spirit. Equally, it can be seen as the recognition of man's lost animal nature and the reconciliation of the male and female archetypes of the animus or anima within the unconscious or as a reiteration of the achievement of balance between the Chinese male and female principles of Yang and Yin fundamental to bodily and spiritual health.

Animals have been an ever present subject throughout the history of art. The very earliest surviving paintings are all of animals and are known from paintings on cave walls in an area called the Franco-Cantabrian triangle of northern Spain and southern France, of which the best known are those at Lascaux and Altamira which date from a period about 18,000–15,000 BC. As society evolved and civilizations sprang up animals continued to be depicted in art. Many characters from one of the first written languages – hieroglyphics – are representations of animals. The largest works of art ever made are the giant animals described on the pampa in present-day Peru, which date from prehistoric times.

With the arrival of the Christian era the story of Noah's Ark captured the imagination of countless artists and it has been a popular theme of western art for hundreds of years. An early example can be found in the frescoes by the fourteenth-century Sienese master Bartolo di Fredi in the Collegiate Church of San Gimignano and a later one in 'The Animals Going Into the Ark' by the sixteenth-century Venetian, Jacopo Bassano, who was an early specialist in painting animals as was his near contemporary Jan Bruegel in the Netherlands who, among many others, also painted this subject. Probably the most evocative and, to my mind, the most charming painting of Noah's Ark is that painted in 1846 by the American, Edward Hicks. Hicks, who lived and worked in Pennsylvania in the late eighteenth and early nineteenth centuries, was a Quaker preacher who painted in his spare time and is regarded today as one of the world's greatest naive artists.

Possibly the earliest analytical study of this story was made in *Arca Noë*, published in 1673 by the German scientist Athanasius Kircher. He precisely dated the flood at 2396 BC. He suggested that the animals were disposed aboard the Ark with the upper storey housing the birds and human living quarters (we know from the Bible that the crew numbered eight), the middle storey the stores and provisions and the lower storey the quadrupeds. The serpents, no doubt on account of their previous misbehaviour in the Garden of Eden, were wisely left to their own devices in the bilge. Kircher explained the absence of any other creatures by restating the received wisdom of the age that 'insects' – which in seventeenth-century terminology included such creatures as frogs, mice and scorpions – did not reproduce in the conventional manner but rather by depositing their seed in rotting carcasses or on vegetation, which was then eaten by other creatures and subsequently expelled as dung from which they hatched. There can have been no shortage of this last substance aboard the Ark. Kircher also lists the animals that were excluded from the Ark, which numbered fabulous beasts such as mermaids, gryphons, manticores, unicorns and giants as well as the equally mythical hybrids. These included the cameleopard, fruit of the mating of the panther and the camel, the hippardium from the panther and horse, the allopecopithicum from the fox and the monkey and the armadillo from the hedgehog and the tortoise.

In the Bible the animals are simply categorized as beasts, cattle, creeping things, fowl and birds. Today the demands of science are more exacting and all life on earth is classified according to the Linnaean system, which was formulated in the 1750s by the Swedish naturalist and founder of taxonomy Carl von Linné (called Carolus Linnaeus). This universal system is a precise method of classifying a living organism by the use of two Latinized words indicating the genus and species. The complete hierarchical system lists as many as twenty

'Noah's Ark' by Edward Hicks, 1846. The animals enter the Ark as the deluge approaches over nineteenth-century Pennsylvania

categories or ranks but normally only seven of these are used. For example you and I – Homo sapiens both – are progressively classified as follows:

KINGDOM *Animalia*

PHYLUM *Chordata*

CLASS *Mammalia*

ORDER *Primates*

FAMILY *Hominidae*

GENUS *Homo*

SPECIES *Homo sapiens*

Put simply, the first of these ranks identifies us as belonging to the animal kingdom together with creatures as simple as single-celled protozoans while the second places us in the same phylum as other vertebrates such as the birds, fish and reptiles. The class specifies the features we share with all other warm-blooded mammals and the order with our near relatives the lemurs, monkeys and apes. The fifth rank identifies us as descendants of the family that included our now extinct hominid ancestors, the genus as human and the last specifically classifies us as modern man, regardless of our race, skin colour or nationality.

The animals that Noah collected together for his Ark would have been very different from those we know today. For instance, there would have been far fewer types of dogs as most of the dozens of breeds that we recognize now are the result of deliberate breeding in relatively recent times. These all share the same Latin name as they are all capable of interbreeding and producing fertile progeny. Some taxonomists even suggest that wolves and domestic dogs should share the same name as their genetic relationship is almost identical. To complicate matters further, quite apart from the domestic animals, there are more than a million extant wild species so far described – the vast majority

'The Animals Entering The Ark' by Bartolo di Fredi, 1367. A detail from the frescoes that depicts fanciful, as well as recognizable, creatures

comprising insects – with, even by the most modest estimate, several times that number waiting to be discovered. Relatively few of these would have been familiar to Noah.

Certain creatures such as the crocodile and the tuatara have remained unchanged since even before the era of the dinosaurs but most have modified their appearance by the process of evolution. It seems probable that the giraffe evolved its extraordinarily long neck over millions of years as a result of browsing on ever higher branches of trees out of reach of its competitors. Yet other creatures have come to occupy particular nîches in the ecosystem in a similar fashion by a process of natural selection, whereby those best suited to survival in their habitat thrive, while those less suited adapt to a different one by gradually acquiring new characteristics – a longer bill, thicker fur, better camouflage – until they ultimately become a separate species.

Those that cannot adapt perish, and throughout time species have become extinct as climates or habitations change. One day all species as we presently know them, including ourselves, will become extinct just as countless species in the past have done. This is a perfectly natural process but one that has sadly been aggravated in historical times by the intervention of man and his seemingly ruthless exploitation and fouling of the planet. Scientific estimates put the current rate of extinctions as between five species per day and one species per *hour*. Either figure is shameful.

Of course, nowadays with our scientific view of the natural world, the story of Noah and his Ark raises many questions. I am about to ask one more, but one that is not directly connected with either theology or zoology and that is specific to the large painting reproduced in the pages of this book. As you can see, in this canvas I have departed from a literal or traditional interpretation of the story –

though you will be able to find one direct visual reference to the original legend – and I have depicted, in various ways, 707 creatures. I have included fish (which presumably had no difficulty in coping with a deluge, no matter how cataclysmic) and insects, neither of which are directly mentioned in the Bible. In line with the original story, 353 of them are each painted twice*, once for each sex, but a single creature is depicted alone and without a mate. The deceptively simple mystery bound up in this painting is to find and name this solitary beast, which is among those listed in the accompanying text, and thereby to restore balance and harmony to the small world represented in my canvas.

I have had this picture reproduced divided up as sixteen details – one to a page – which some people may care to separate from the binding and reconstitute as a single image nearer to its original size. This may well make some of the couples appear clearer. A careful study of the text will prove instructive and, to help you, I have given some cryptic written guidance or ways of beginning to explore the picture facing each whole page detail. From then on you must use your eyes to track down the fugitive.

So there you have it. On the surface this book might seem to be the simplest of puzzles and certainly one that is fun and accessible to everyone, no matter what their age, educational background or nationality. But, as I have learned afresh in creating it, just like the interrelationships of the animal kingdom and the intricacies of the Bible story, what may seem simple at first glance often assumes Byzantine complexity when looked into more deeply. The few creatures represented in my painting are but a barely audible whisper

'The Animals Going Into The Ark' by Jacopo Bassano. A detail from one of Bassano's Noah's Arks

compared to the tumultuous anthem that nature is singing. To me not the least amusing aspect of this book is that, when all is said and done, these 'animals' are, in fact, no more than paint stains on a piece of canvas – an artist's sleight of hand.

Besides being designed to baffle, bemuse, bedevil, befuddle and generally drive you to distraction, *The Ultimate Noah's Ark* continues a theme common to all of my work – that of seeing. By seeing, I mean using the innate intelligence of one's eyes to understand what one is looking at. So by looking at, and above all *seeing*, the myriad images contained in this picture – and ultimately even 'seeing' what is *not* there – you will be making a visual journey unconfined by either time or space. I sincerely hope it will be a delight for its own sake and that it may even lead you on to a more tangible treasure.

Good hunting!

* AUTHOR'S NOTE

Anyone already familiar with my work will be expecting to find the image of a snail somewhere in the canvas. This ponderous creature is symbolic of the amount of time that my paintbrush takes to cover an area and has become a kind of motif. In this painting the snail appears sixteen times altogether, contrived in such a way that it can be found once in each whole-page detail of the painting. This is the one and only mollusc that I have included and should not be counted in the total indicated above.

INSECTS, ARACHNIDS & MYRIAPODS

The class Insecta (or Hexapoda) forms the largest group of living creatures on the planet. It comprises 83 per cent of all described animal life and there are almost 1 million known species. But new species are constantly being discovered and entomologists have recently estimated that there could be as many as 25–30 million living species. The number of individual insects is equally astounding with a generally accepted estimate of 10,000 million insects to each square km (26,000 million per square mile)!

Insects are defined as invertebrates with external skeletons (exoskeletons) that are periodically discarded as they grow, jointed limbs, segmented bodies, six legs and (usually) wings. Certain insects, such as butterflies and moths, undergo distinct changes in form (metamorphosis) as they grow from egg to larva and finally to imago or adulthood by way of a dormant period as a pupa. Arachnids share some of the features of insects, but lack wings and possess eight legs. Myriapods are commonly thought of as insects but are, in fact, a separate class consisting of about 11,000 species, including centipedes and millipedes.

The smallest insects are a certain species of parasitic wasp known as Fairy Flies (family Mymaridae) the tiniest of which is barely 0.21mm (0.008in) long and therefore all but invisible to the naked eye. The smallest arachnid, appropriately a mite, is barely half this size. A competition for the giant among insects might be won by the Atlas Moth *Attacus atlas*, which has a wingspan of more than 25.5cm (about 10in).

Insects generally come to our attention only as pests and some, such as the malarial Mosquito *Anopheles gambiae*, the plague-carrying Oriental Rat Flea *Xenopsylla cheopis* or the Tsetse Fly *Glossina brevipalpis*, known to transmit sleeping sickness, are positively dangerous on a large scale. A few, such as the Silkworm *Bombyx mori* and the Honey-bee *Apis mellifera*, are actively encouraged by man.

Bee-eating Beetle or Chequered Beetle
Trichodes apiarius

The larvae of the Bee-eating Beetle live with wild bees, including honey-bees, on which they prey. Also known as Chequered Beetles because of the distinctive patterning of their wing-case or elytra, the adults grow to 9–16mm (0.4–0.6in) long and can be seen in the summer on umbelliferous flowers. These beetles have become increasingly rare during this century in many parts of their range, in central and southern Europe.

Brimstone Butterfly *Gonepteryx rhamni*

Brimstone is the old name for sulphur and refers to the yellow colouring of this butterfly, though the female is paler and much less conspicuous than the more brilliantly coloured male. It ranges from Siberia to northern Africa and is to be seen in submontane and lowland habitats and especially in lightly wooded areas that contain buckthorn on which the caterpillars feed. A single generation is produced each year. The adults hibernate and are first seen on the wing in early spring. The wingspan of this species is 50–55mm (1.95–2.14in).

Bumble Bee or Humble Bee *Bombus terrestris*

The familiar Bumble Bees, of which *B. terrestris* is an example, are natives of the temperate regions of the world. *B. terrestris* has been introduced to Australasia. Throughout their range these robust, hairy insects, which have an average size of 1.5–2.5cm (about 0.6–1in), do a splendid job in the pollination of flowers. They collect pollen on the stiff hairs, known as 'pollen baskets', on their hindlegs. Bumble Bees make their nests in or on the surface of the ground, often occupying deserted bird or mouse nests, where in spring the queen begins to lay the eggs that will produce the colony. This colony lasts for the summer months after which the workers die and new queens leave the nest to mate and afterwards hibernate to begin anew the following year. The common collective name of these social bees is onomatopoeic, derived from the lazy humming sound that they make as they fly.

Camberwell Beauty or Mourning Cloak
Nymphalis antiopa

This butterfly ranges across most of Europe and Asia, as well as North America where it is known as the Mourning Cloak. It can also be found in parts of Central America. Camberwell is in London, England, but this species is, in fact, a rarity there. A single generation is produced each year and the adults, which measure 55–75mm (2.1–2.9in), are on the wing from June and July onwards. After emerging from hibernation they breed and from March–June the larvae can be seen feeding on the leaves of aspen, poplar, willow and birch. In years when large populations are produced these caterpillars are capable of completely defoliating such trees.

Cardinal Beetle *Pyrochroa coccinea*

Cardinal Beetles with their brightly coloured elytra are named after the traditional scarlet robes of Roman Catholic cardinals. *P. coccinea* is the largest of only 3 species found in Europe and grows to 14–18mm (0.5–0.7in). The larvae are found beneath the bark of trees and feed on small insects, sometimes resorting to cannibalism if these are scarce. The adult beetles live mainly on woodland flowers and shrubs.

Centipede *Scolopendra cingulata*

Although their name suggests that they have 100 legs, Centipedes can have anything from 14–177 pairs of legs. Worldwide there are about 2800 species. *S. cingulata* is a smaller – 9cm (3.5in) – member of the order Scolopendrida; it is found in the warmer parts of the world and can inflict painful bites with its venomous, jaw-like claws situated just behind the head. It has 21–23 pairs of legs and lives in cracks and holes in dry, stony places where it preys on other tiny invertebrates.

Cicada *Tibicina haematodes*

Unlike grasshoppers and crickets, which produce their sound by the stridulation of their legs and wings, Cicadas sing by repeatedly distorting their membranous tymbals located in their abdomen. This produces a loud, prolonged series of rapid clicks – between 100–500 a second – that can sometimes be heard for up to 1km (0.6 mile). The sound, which is specific to each of the more than 2000 species, is made only by the males and is associated with congregation, courtship or alarm. In China males are caged and kept like songbirds. After the eggs hatch, the larvae live underground feeding on the xylem sap from plant roots and take a long time to grow. Cicadas live in wooded habitats and *T. haematodes* grows to 4cm (1.57in).

Colorado Beetle or Potato Bug
Leptinotarsa decemlineata

A serious worldwide agricultural pest, the Colorado Beetle originated in the Rocky Mountains of North America where its natural food was a species of nightshade known as Buffalo Burr *Solanum rostratum*. As the early pioneers moved west they took the potato with them and when they reached Colorado the beetle changed its diet to the more abundant potato and rapidly multiplied to plague proportions. It soon spread back east at a rate of 135km (nearly 84 miles) a year and from there it was only a matter of time before it reached Europe and the rest of the world. The exceptionally hardy beetle hibernates underground and emerges in late spring to lay eggs on potato leaves. Up to three generations are produced each year, depending on the climate. The adult measures 10mm (0.4in).

Common Earwig *Forficula auricularia*

The curious common name of this widespread insect is the same in many languages, such as *Perce-oreille* in French and *Ohrwurm* in German. The English term can be traced from the Old English 'ēarwicga' through Middle English 'arwygyll' to its modern name. These all seem to suggest, mistakenly, the predilection of this nocturnal crevice-dweller to wriggle into sleeping people's ears, though it has undoubtedly done so occasionally. This association is perpetuated in an old folk remedy that prescribes dried, powdered earwig mixed with hare's urine as a cure for deafness. The Latin name *Forficula* (little scissors) alludes to the pincers (*cerci*) on its tail; those of the males are curved and the females straight. Common Earwigs have large wings that are rarely seen. They eat both plant matter and lice. They hibernate underground and in spring the female lays 20–50 eggs, which hatch as nymphs and eventually attain an adult size of about 20–25mm (0.8–nearly 1in).

♂♀ Emperor Dragonfly *Anax imperator*

The 5000 present-day species of dragonfly are the descendants of similar flying insects that existed about 300 million years ago. The fossil record shows a giant dragonfly-like insect, *Meganeura monyi*, with a wingspan of 70cm (27.5in) – the largest insect ever known. Emperor Dragonflies, however, only grow to 8cm (3.2in) and belong to a group commonly known as 'hawkers'. Dragonflies are swift, powerful flyers – perhaps attaining speeds of up to 29km/h (18mph) – and voracious feeders capable of eating 14 per cent of their body weight a day, of insects such as mosquitos and midges. Their prey are located with large, compound eyes, which have 30,000 facets that can detect movement at 20–40m (65–131ft). Eggs are laid in the stems and leaves of aquatic plants and hatch as aquatic larvae, which are opportunistic hunters eating a wide variety of small underwater creatures. In Sumatra these larvae are considered a gastronomic delicacy and in China are used medicinally. After 1 or 2 years in this larval stage the dragonfly emerges from the water and assumes its adult form after a final moult, becoming sexually mature 1–2 weeks later.

♂♀ Garden Tiger Moth *Arctia caja*

This gaudy moth is distributed throughout Europe, Asia and North America and can be found in abundance in agricultural land up to elevations in excess of 600m (over 1968ft). The adult male has a wingspan of 45–65mm (1.75–2.5in), though those of the female are slightly larger. The colour and pattern of the markings are as individual as fingerprints. The polyphagous larvae are popularly known as 'woolly bears'. Their long, irritant hairs are a deterrent to most birds that might eat them. The annual generation takes to the wing from June–August.

♂♀ Magpie Moth *Abraxas grossulariata*

Hazel, peach, blackthorn and especially currant and gooseberry are the principal food plants for the caterpillars of this species, which often become a serious pest. But due to the increased use of pesticides this once abundant species has decreased dramatically in certain parts of its range during this century. The species is distributed throughout the Palaearctic as far east as Japan. The young larvae hibernate, then recommence feeding the following spring and metamorphose into adult

moths that fly from June–August. The wingspan is up to 45mm (1.75in).

♂♀ Migratory Locust *Locusta migratoria*

Locusts are short-horned grasshoppers that periodically migrate great distances in vast, voracious swarms. One such swarm in 1889 was calculated to cover 3220 square km (2000 square miles), and to consist of many thousands of millions of insects. Locusts seem to undergo 2 distinct phases: a harmless solitary one when the insects are camouflaged and – when climatic conditions are right and population density increases – a destructive gregarious one when they attain a brighter coloration and migrate. Collectively, such swarms have gargantuan appetites capable of devastating the agriculture of whole continents if left unchecked and are only stopped by adverse weather conditions or, today, by the use of pesticides. The range of the Migratory Locust includes Africa, much of Eurasia, Australasia and the East Indies and the average adult size is 6cm (2.4in).

♂♀ Monarch or Milkweed or Wanderer *Danaus plexippus*

Although it is most often known as the Monarch, Wanderer is perhaps the most fitting of the common names applied to this native American butterfly, which migrates annually for distances of up to 2900km (1800 miles). It has now become established in parts of southern Europe, the Pacific Islands, Australia and New Zealand. In America the caterpillars feed on the poisonous Milkweed plants *Asclepias syriaca*, *A. curassavica* and *A. incarnata* and the toxins are retained by the insect, which gives due warning to would-be predators by its bold patterning and coloration. Monarchs measure 85–95mm (3.3–3.7in).

♂♀ Musk Beetle *Aromia moschata*

The Musk Beetle – so-called because of its musky smell – belongs to a group commonly known as 'longhorn' or 'longicorn' beetles, because of their exceptionally long antennae. It is the sole member of its genus to be found in Europe where it is widely distributed. It can be seen on flowers and in larval form on willows and occasionally on alders and poplars. Large numbers of larvae constitute a pest, though this species is far less common than in bygone days. Musk Beetles grow up to 34mm (1.3in) long.

♂♀ Puss Moth *Cerura vinula*

As a caterpillar the Puss Moth has three lines of defence. Firstly, its coloration and patterning tend to break up its outline in a form of disruptive camouflage that makes it difficult for a predator to distinguish. If this fails it adopts a defensive posture, displaying its facial markings, which include spots that turn its frontal aspect into a huge, terrifying 'face' with whip-like tails. As a final deterrent it sprays formic acid at its aggressor from its

thoracic glands. Puss Moths are found abundantly in damp habitats throughout the entire temperate Palaearctic region and at altitudes of up to 2500m (over 8202ft). They hibernate as pupae and are on the wing from April–July, depending on the latitude. The larvae feed on willows and poplar and the adult moths grow to 45–75mm (1.75–2.92in).

♂♀ Red Admiral *Vanessa atalanta*

The home of this common butterfly is northern Africa and southern Europe; its range extends east to Central Asia, but it migrates throughout Europe during the year. It also occurs in North America and measures about 50–60mm (1.9–2.3in). After hatching from their eggs, the solitary caterpillars feed on nettle leaves before pupating and subsequently emerging at the end of summer to feed on overripe fruit in orchards. They are especially fond of pears and plums. Red Admirals remain until late autumn, but normally only those south of the Alps successfully hibernate.

♂♀ Scarce Swallowtail *Iphiclides podalirius*

This butterfly gets its common name in a rather Anglo-centric way due to its rarity in the British Isles where it is doubtful if it has ever been resident. In parts of the rest of its range, which includes southern Europe, North Africa, Asia Minor, Transcaucasia and western China, it is, relatively speaking, more abundant, though it is a protected species in some countries. It inhabits forest and steppe areas and is most often found near blackthorn, hawthorn, rowan and cultivated fruit trees on which the caterpillars feed. Depending on the climate 2 or 3 generations are produced annually. Adults fly from April–September and reach a size of 50–70mm (nearly 2–2.7in).

♂♀ Scorpion *Euscorpius flavicaudis*

The 1200 species of Scorpion live in the tropics, deserts and the warmer regions of the world. The Scorpion's sting is located at the tip of its tail and is supplied by 2 large venom glands, which are of 2 types. In the most dangerous scorpions – like the deadly Mexican Durango Scorpion *Centruoides suffusus* – which all belong to the family Buthidae, the venom is a neurotoxin that usually causes death. The sting of the 35mm (1.4in) *E. flavicaudis*, which is often found in southern Europe, is milder as its effect is localized and is reportedly like a severe wasp sting. Scorpions feed on insects and spiders, which they run down and grasp with their claw-like pincers or pedipalps and then tear apart with their small chelicerae situated near their mouthparts. Only larger prey is stung to paralyse it. After indirect fertilization takes place, the female scorpion often devours her mate and the eggs are carried within her body and born live, 1 or 2 at a time over several weeks. They travel on their mother's back for a further week. A Scorpion *Palaeophonus nuncius* existed 400 million years ago, which makes it the oldest known arachnid.

The carnival commences and 707 animals have gathered to celebrate.
There are 353 different creatures each accompanied by their mate,
but one among them came all alone. Name this lonely creature
and you could win the prize.

There are also sixteen snails, one in each of the whole-page details of this painting that follow.
These molluscs are over and above the creatures listed in the text and need not be counted.
But if you can find them you will be looking in just the kind of way necessary
to solve this riddle.

♂♀ Seven-spot Ladybird
♀ *Coccinella septempunctata*

Ladybirds are more properly known as ladybugs in North America and the various species may be identified by the number of spots on their elytra. One of the most familiar of beetles, their vivid colouring is a warning to potential predators of their disagreeable taste. Several generations are produced each year and both the larvae and the adults are voracious predators of aphids, scale insects and other pests, which makes them a valuable alternative to pesticides. Some species have been specially bred to be introduced into orchards. Their common name originated in medieval Europe as 'beetles of Our Lady', when they were used in medicinal folk remedies against toothache, measles and colic. Seven-spot Ladybirds are common throughout Europe and grow to 5–8mm (0.2–0.3in).

♂♀ Spider Beetle *Sphaericus gibboides*

At first sight this small, wingless beetle can be mistaken for a spider. It is a native of North America where its relatives, the White-marked Spider Beetle *Ptinus fur* and the American Spider Beetle *Mezium americanum*, are noted household pests. In recent years the opportunist Spider Beetle has arrived in the coastal towns of Britain, France, Holland and Germany, after crossing the Atlantic in grain-carrying ships, the cargo of which has sustained it on its voyage. These nocturnal beetles reach an adult size of only 1.3–2.7m (0.05–0.1in).

♂♀ Tarantula *Avicularia avicularia*

Tarantula is the common name for many species of spider found in the tropical forests and plantations of South America. The Tarantula feeds on small mammals, reptiles, amphibians, insects and small birds such as hummingbirds. Most people react with revulsion to its hairy body, large fangs and enormous size – it measures 19cm (nearly 7.5in) across, including its legs, but its body is about 6cm (2.3in) long. Its highly irritant hairs are its principal defence while its venom is relatively weak. It relies on its great strength to run down and overpower its prey, which it injects with powerful digestive juices, then its fangs suck out the liquified matter. After mating – a dangerous experience for the male as he is sometimes devoured by his mate after copulation – the female of this nocturnal species lays 100–200 eggs in a cocoon inside a tube-shaped web. The young emerge 20 days later.

FISH

Fishes are mostly cold-blooded vertebrates with fins and scales; they breathe through gills and spend most or all of their time beneath water. Fishes account for over half of the vertebrates that currently exist and there are more than 23,000 known species. New species are constantly being discovered and described. Fishes can be as small as the Philippine Goby *Pandaka pygmaea*, which is 10mm (0.4in) long with a weight of 1.5g (0.5oz), or giants such as the Whale Shark *Rhincodon typus*, which has a length of as much as 18m (59ft) and a weight of up to 43 tonnes (94,815lb). Fishes inhabit waters ranging from thermal springs, where the temperature is as high as 42°C (107.6°F), to numbing Arctic waters with temperatures below 0°C (32°F), and from high mountain streams to the darkness and unimaginable pressures of the deep sea.

♂♀ Alewife *Alosa pseudoharengus*

The Alewife is a member of the herring family (Clupeidae) and an important food fish of North America. There are 2 populations: one is marine and enters rivers to spawn, and the other spends its whole life in freshwater, including the Great Lakes. Saltwater Alewives begin their breeding migration in March and, after laying their eggs in sluggish streams or ponds, they return to the ocean no later than May. The marine form attains lengths of 38cm (14.9in) while the freshwater one only reaches about 19cm (7.4in). The principal food of the Alewife is plankton and small fish.

♂♀ Archerfish *Toxotes jaculator*

This is one of the 5 species of Archerfish, so named because of their ability to 'shoot' insect prey down from overhanging vegetation by forcibly expelling drops of water from the mouth. The tongue is positioned against the roof of the mouth to form a narrow tube that acts rather like a gun barrel. The power for this spitting mechanism comes from the compression of water in the gill cavity of the fish by means of muscle action and the drops are propelled with considerable strength and accuracy to hit targets up to 1.5m (4.9ft) away. In aiming its shots the fish must compensate for the refraction of light at the surface of the water. *T. jaculator* is found in rivers and estuaries from northern Australia west to the Persian Gulf and reaches a length of 23cm (9in).

♂♀ Atlantic Flyingfish *Cypselurus heterurus*

The so-called 'wings' of this fish are, in fact, expanded pectoral and pelvic fins that enable it to glide, rather than truly fly, for considerable distances after propelling itself along on the surface of the water. While still beneath the surface it uses its powerful tail with its fins folded close to its body to achieve thrust. It then leaps clear, extends its fins and glides for up to 100m (328ft), about 1.5m (nearly 5ft) above the surface. Such a flight usually lasts around 10 seconds. Flight times vary depending on prevailing winds. Sometimes the fish is carried quite high and some individuals crash on to the decks of ships. Atlantic Flyingfish grow as long as 43cm (nearly 17in) and are found in the temperate and tropical waters of the North Atlantic Ocean – but rarely north of 55° – and the Mediterranean Sea.

♂♀ Atlantic Salmon *Salmo salar*

Today the flesh of the Atlantic Salmon is considered a delicacy and carries an appropriately high price, but in the nineteenth century it was, like the oyster, a food for the poor. Atlantic Salmon are migratory fishes that spend part of their adult lives in the sea but return to breed in the rivers where they hatched. They locate these rivers by smell. After swimming upriver past many obstacles they spawn there. The male fertilizes the eggs that the female has laid in a shallow nest called a 'redd' excavated in the gravel of the riverbed. During this time the fish do not feed. The eggs hatch the following spring and the young spend 1–4 years in the river before going to sea and returning 1–4 years later to spawn. Atlantic Salmon are found on both sides of the ocean as far south as northern Spain and when fully grown measure 1.5m (4.9ft).

♂♀ Bluefish *Pomatomus saltatrix*

The Bluefish inhabits the warm and tropical coastal waters and open seas of the Atlantic and Indian Oceans where it is a voracious predator of smaller marine animals and fish, often killing more than it can eat. It is an important game and food fish that travels in shoals and grows to lengths of 1.2m (3.9ft).

♂♀ Blue Shark *Prionace glauca*

Like all sharks and rays, the Blue Shark is a cartilaginous fish that lacks true bone and instead has a skeleton consisting of cartilage. This class of fishes also has no scales, and the skin bears minute but densely packed, enamel-covered dermal denticles that feel like sandpaper to the touch. This roughened skin is known as 'shagreen' when cured. A further peculiarity of these fish is that they do not possess swim-bladders, which most other orders of fish use for buoyancy, so they tend to remain in constant motion to avoid sinking. Blue Sharks are pelagic and occur in all temperate and tropical seas often undertaking long migrations to warmer waters during the winter months. A typical Blue Shark measures 3.5m (11.5ft) and might grow to 4m (over 13ft). Blue Sharks are viviparous and give birth to between 25–50 young, which each measure 35–45cm (13.8-17.7in) at birth. Their principal diet is shoaling fish such as herring, pilchard and mackerel. Though they are rightly regarded as dangerous to man such attacks are rare.

♂♀ Boarfish *Capros aper*

The Boarfish lives at depths of between 100–400m (roughly 328–1312ft) in the warmer open waters of the eastern Atlantic Ocean from Ireland south to Senegal and in the Mediterranean Sea. It grows to 10–16cm (3.9–6.3in) and has a protrusible jaw. It is covered with tiny toothed scales that make it feel rough to the touch. Spawning takes place each summer resulting in free-floating eggs. The diet of the Boarfish is marine worms, molluscs and small crustaceans.

♂♀ Cod *Gadus morhua*

An indication of how man has exploited this valuable food fish is that a century ago Cod of up to 90kg (198.4lb) were landed while today the average fish caught is only 4.5kg (9.9lb), though there are rare 20-year-old 'giants' of 18kg (39.6lb). A typical Cod measures about 1.2m (3.9ft). Spawning occurs in the North Atlantic between February and April and each female produces up to 5 million fertilized eggs, which are left to drift in the ocean currents where barely one in a million is believed to survive. Cod feed on smaller fish, worms, molluscs and crustaceans. As well as for their flesh Cod are used for their roe, their internal organs, which are processed into fish meal, and the oil of their liver, which is especially rich in vitamins A and D.

♂♀ Coney *Cephalopholis fulvus*

The Coney is the most numerous member of the grouper family – Serranidae – which is a part of the largest and most varied order of fishes, the Perciformes, comprising 150 families and 7791 known species. Conies grow to 30cm (11.8in) long and inhabit the coastal waters and coral reefs of the western Atlantic Ocean from Florida throughout the Caribbean and as far south as Brazil. They feed mainly on crustaceans and are an important food fish.

♂♀ Dolphin or Dolphinfish or Dorado *Coryphaena hippurus*

This true fish should not be confused with the well known group of aquatic mammals also called dolphins. The colourful and swift Dolphinfish is highly prized by game fishermen and its flesh is regarded as delicious. The Dolphinfish is pelagic and can be found in temperate and tropical waters throughout the world either alone or in schools. Although the sexes are similar in appearance, the male is considerably larger than the female and attains lengths of 1.5m (4.9ft). This carnivore feeds on a variety of fish as well as squid and crustaceans and is reputedly fond of flyingfish, which it chases at speed causing them to leap from the water as they try to escape.

♂♀ Haddock *Melanogrammus aeglefinus*

The Haddock is a bottom-dwelling member of the cod family (Gadidae) and a valuable food fish of the North Atlantic. Its principal diet is worms, molluscs, small fish and brittlestars and it spawns from March–June. Each female produces up to a million eggs that are left to drift on the surface before hatching as 5mm (0.2in) larvae. An adult Haddock measures up to 1m (3.3ft).

♂♀ Hake *Merluccius merluccius*

Although its flesh is not as highly prized, this is another commercially valuable relative of the cod. The Hake is a swift carnivore that grows to lengths of 1.1m (3.6ft). During the day it lives near the bottom, but each night rises to midwater to feed on squid and small fishes. After spawning takes place in spring or summer, the eggs rise to the surface where they are driven by the wind, the direction of which – whether towards or away from the rich inshore feeding grounds – determines the size of the next generation.

♂♀ John Dory *Zeus faber*

St Peter once withdrew a gold piece from the mouth of the John Dory and today the two marks left by his fingers where he gripped the fish can be clearly seen on either side of its body – or so the legend goes. The John Dory's common name is possibly a corruption of the Italian *janitore* (doorkeeper) or is derived from the French *jaune dorée* (yellow-gold) or perhaps *jaune d'orée* (yellow-bordered) for its coloration. The maximum adult size of its tall, laterally flattened body is about 66cm (26in). It is to be found in eastern Atlantic coastal waters from southern Norway south to the Cape of Good Hope as well as the Mediterranean. The breeding season is in the spring and summer. It feeds on smaller fish that it approaches stealthily, then shoots forward its protrusile mouth to grasp its prey.

♂♀ Mackerel *Scomber scombrus*

This is an abundant species that is often found in huge schools during the summer months when spawning takes place. The female produces up to 450,000 eggs, which float freely until they hatch. Mackerel are predatory, feeding on small fish and crustaceans, and live in the coastal waters of the Atlantic from the Gulf of St Lawrence to North Carolina in the west and from Iceland and Scandinavia to the Canary Islands in the east. Their main natural enemies are sharks, tunny and dolphins. Mackerel are a very important food fish that can reach lengths of up to 66cm (26in), though most are about half this size when caught.

♂♀ Moorish Idol or Toby *Zanclus canescens*

The common name of this fish is often explained by the story that it is revered by indigenous fishermen and respectfully returned to the water after it has been caught. It is found only in the Indian and Pacific Oceans where it inhabits coral reefs, the boldly patterned markings possibly acting as disruptive camouflage that makes it harder for a predator to define. This is probably accentuated by its extended dorsal fin. A fully grown specimen measures 18cm (7in).

♂♀ Sardine or Pilchard *Sardina pilchardus*

Sardines are to be found in the eastern Atlantic between the west coast of Ireland and southern Morocco where they spawn in the spring. They are also found in the Mediterranean where they breed all year round laying about 50,000 eggs, which hatch into larvae 4mm (0.2in) long. A 15-year-old Sardine can attain a length of 26cm (10.2in). This smaller relative of the herring is an important food fish whether fresh, canned or salted and is also a valuable source of oil.

♂♀ Siamese Fighting Fish *Betta splendens*

The natural home of this popular aquarium fish is the stagnant ponds and ditches and slow-moving freshwater streams of Thailand. The long-finned males of this species, which grow to about 6.5cm (2.6in), are well known for their aggression towards each other. In the wild this behaviour is ritualized but in captivity fights are often staged for gambling. Their natural diet is the larvae of mosquitos and other aquatic insects. Before mating the male builds a raft of air bubbles. He glues the fertilized eggs laid by his mate to the underside of the raft with mucus and guards them until they hatch. They grow rapidly but only live for about 2 years. The females do not possess the extravagant fins and colouring of the males.

♂♀ Smooth Hammerhead Shark *Sphyrna zygaena*

The most notable feature of this highly predaceous and dangerous shark is its large, laterally expanded head from which it derives its common name. The purpose of this strange shape seems unclear but some experts think that the spacing of its eyes and nostrils so far apart improves its depth-perception and the ability to locate prey by smell. Others believe that its electro-reception system – an electrically sensitive system of pits and channels found in the head, and known as the 'ampullae of Lorenzini' – is enhanced. This swift, powerful creature feeds on fish, rays and other sharks and is found in tropical and warm temperate coastal and inshore waters worldwide, migrating to cooler waters in summer. Adults reach a length of about 4.3m (14.1ft).

♂♀ Snapper *Chrysophrys auratus*

This is a valuable food fish throughout its range, which includes the western Pacific Ocean, the coasts of Australia and New Zealand and Lord Howe Island. When young it lives in large schools close to the shore and as it matures it frequents deeper waters where it feeds on smaller fishes and hard-shelled invertebrates. It attains a maximum length of 1.3m (4.3ft).

♂♀ Swordfish *Xiphias gladius*

The streamlined Swordfish is the only member of the Xiphiidae family. The sword-like snout of this solitary creature takes up to a third of its total body length, which is as much as 4.9m (16ft). The sharp, flattened 'sword' is used to lash the water when the fish is feeding on its preferred diet of saury, mackerel, herring, flying fish and squid, but it remains unclear whether this action is to lacerate the prey or simply to disorientate it. Its great strength, which enables it to swim at speeds of up to 56–64km/h (35–40mph), and its maximum weight of 450g (more than 992lb) make it a highly prized game fish and its flesh is considered a great delicacy. There have been numerous reports of Swordfish

I have painted at least one couple among the creatures
featured in the detail opposite. If you can name them
you will have only another 352 pairs to find. Also look out for
a high-flyer with mountainous connections, a regally furred creature,
an airborne warship, a dweller among rhododendrons and the provider
of a vital ingredient for a pizza. If you compare this picture
with the next you may well find some companions to one or more
of the animals featured here. Can you see the snail?

attacking boats and in one well-documented case a wooden hull was pierced to a depth of 56cm (22in).

♂♀ Tarpon *Tarpon atlanticus*

The great strength of the Tarpon makes it a much prized game fish. It is a large fish that grows to 1.2–2.4m (3.9–7.8ft); it has large, silvery scales. It is a voracious predator of smaller fish and crabs and a female can lay as many as 12 million eggs in the open sea. The larvae develop in inshore waters, swamps and estuaries. The Tarpon is to be found in the Atlantic Ocean from Nova Scotia in the north to Brazil and West Africa in the south.

♂♀ Yellowfin Tuna *Thunnus albacares*

The Yellowfin Tuna, like the other species of tuna fish, is of great commercial value as food and is to be found in all tropical and warm temperate seas. In summer it swims near the surface but in winter it inhabits depths of 30–180m (98.4–590ft). Yellowfin Tunas migrate each season as they are intolerant of temperatures below about 10°C (50°F). They travel in shoals but old specimens, which grow to 2m (6.6ft), are often solitary. Their chief diet is squid and other shoaling fish such as herring and mackerel and their chief predator, apart from man who takes them in large numbers, is the Killer Whale *Orcinus orca*.

AMPHIBIANS

The amphibians were the first creatures to emerge from the sea and colonize the land about 375–350 million years ago. Most modern amphibians still need to live near water where they must return to breed. They can be defined as air-breathing, hairless, featherless, cold-blooded vertebrates with soft, glandular skins. Their eggs are usually laid in water and they typically go through an aquatic larval stage. Of the approximately 3500 extant species, the smallest is a tiny toad from Brazil, *Psyllophryne didactylus*, which measures just 0.6mm (0.3in). The largest is the Japanese Giant Salamander *Andrias japonicus*, which can attain lengths of 180cm (70.9in) and weigh 25kg (over 55lb). Amphibians are of little economic importance to man, but in Europe the hindlegs of the Edible Frog *Rana esculenta* are considered a gastronomic delicacy. The deadly skin secretions of the vividly coloured Central and southern American Arrow-poison Frogs *Sminthillus limbatus* are used by the indigenous Indians to tip their hunting arrows.

♂♀ Common Frog *Rana temporaria*

Although superficially similar, frogs differ from toads in that they are agile, smooth-skinned leapers that prefer damp

locations whereas toads are slow, warty-skinned waddlers that seek dry ones. Common Frogs are to be found in moist areas such as ponds, freshwater swamps and marshes throughout Scandinavia, Europe – excluding Spain and Italy – and east into Asia and Japan. Their coloration is variable, they typically measure about 10cm (3.9in) and their diet consists mainly of various arthropods. After mating takes place from February–April the female lays 3000–4000 eggs in a jellylike cluster commonly known as frogspawn, which later hatch as tadpoles and metamorphose into frogs after 2–3 months when they are capable of leaving the water. Common Frogs hibernate, some on land and some in the mud beneath water. Heket was the frog-headed goddess of the ancient Egyptians who was one of the patrons of childbirth.

♂♀ Common Toad *Bufo bufo*

At 15cm (5.9in), the female Common Toad is notably larger than the 8cm (3.1in) male. The Common Toad is nocturnal, leaving its resting place each evening to eat vast quantities of earthworms and other invertebrates, especially ants. The breeding season is in March after which the female lays 3000–4000 eggs in fairly deep water in gelatinous strings as long as 5m (16.4ft). These hatch as tiny 5mm (0.2in) tadpoles that metamorphose into toads after 2 months. The Common Toad's adult habitat is predominantly dry and it ranges throughout Europe, northern Africa and Asia as far east as Japan. To deter predators the Common Toad has two crescent-shaped parotid glands located behind the eyes that release a poison if it is molested. This unpleasant exudation irritates the eyes and mucous membranes of its attacker. It also inflates its body by as much as 50 per cent to intimidate a would-be aggressor. It hibernates in dry places from October–February. In medieval Europe, people believed that the toad carried a jewel in its head, which it would eject in a fit of delight if placed on a scarlet cloth. This 'toadstone' was said to change colour if it detected poison and was also thought to be an antidote to snake and wasp venom.

♂♀ Fire Salamander *Salamandra salamandra*

The nocturnal Fire Salamander can be found throughout the temperate regions of Europe, apart from Britain, and north-west Africa as well as in parts of south-west Asia in hilly and mountainous regions, but always near water. It hibernates in those regions where temperatures fall below 0°C (32°F). Its vivid coloration warns would-be predators that it is unpalatable as it has poisonous skin secretions that can even prove fatal to small mammals. It feeds on small invertebrates and measures from 20–28cm (7.8–11in). Mating takes place on dry land in March and April after which the female gives birth to up to 50 live larvae in water that metamorphose into adults after 2–3 months. The mythical lizard-like salamander of legend was supposed to live in fire that it could endure without harm. It is the heraldic emblem of constancy.

♂♀ Oriental Fire-bellied Toad *Bombina orientalis*

Although the camouflage of the top half of its body is its first line of defence, the bright underside of this creature is displayed if it is threatened to warn its attacker of the unpleasant nature of its skin secretions. The home of the Oriental Fire-bellied Toad is the rice fields and mountain streams of Korea, north-east China and parts of eastern Siberia where it feeds on insects, worms and small molluscs. It hibernates from October–April and mating occurs soon after. The female lays 120–200 eggs in clusters of 15–30. These rapidly hatch into tadpoles that mature and leave the water by late August. The females eventually attain a full adult size of 5cm (nearly 2in); the males are rather smaller.

REPTILES

Reptiles, in the form of dinosaurs, were the rulers of the earth for about 135 million years from the middle Triassic period (about 200 million years ago) to the late upper Cretaceous era (about 65 million years ago). They began evolving from amphibians even earlier and were the far distant ancestors of both the birds and the mammals of today. The four extant orders of reptiles are generally defined as cold-blooded, scale-covered vertebrates that reproduce by internal fertilization. Reptiles vary greatly in size; the smallest is probably the *Sphaerodactylus* Gecko at just 36mm (1.4in) and the biggest the Anaconda *Eunectes murinus* (see below), which reaches 9m (29.5ft). Most species of reptiles are to be found in temperate and tropical regions of the world where the ambient temperatures are relatively high and where they can regulate their body temperature, for instance, by exposure to the sun.

♂♀ Anaconda *Eunectes murinus*

The Anaconda is the largest snake and can reach a length of up to 9m (29.5ft) and a weight of 150kg (over 330lb), though its average adult size is probably about 5m (16.4ft). Its home is the tropical rivers of South America east of the Andes and it also occurs in Trinidad. Anacondas catch their prey by lurking in murky water until a young tapir, deer, capybara or other small mammal or bird comes to drink whereupon they seize it and kill it by constriction. They do not need to eat for 2 weeks after a large kill and take up to 7 days to digest this meal. After mating with the male, which makes loud, booming courtship noises, the female produces 20–70 live young, which measure 60–90cm (23.5–35.4in).

♂♀ Asiatic Cobra *Naja naja*

The Asiatic Cobra with its distinctive 'hood' grows to 1.7–2.2m (5.6–7.2ft) and is widely distributed throughout India, Sri Lanka,

Central and south-east Asia. It is highly venomous with sufficient venom to kill 15 people, and these snakes are reportedly responsible for about 20,000 human deaths each year. Eastern populations are also capable of accurately spitting their venom for up to 2m (6.6ft) into their opponent's eyes, which causes severe pain and sometimes results in permanent blindness if not treated promptly. This nocturnal snake eats mainly rats and mice for which it has a huge appetite. It sometimes consumes up to 10 each day and often enters human dwellings in search of them. Following such a feast it does not feed again for 2–3 weeks. After copulation, which involves a mating 'dance' when couples entwine, the female digs a burrow in the earth where 10–20 eggs are laid and guarded until they hatch. The natural enemies of this snake are raptors and the mongoose, which is more agile than the Cobra and has a partial resistance to its venom. Cobras are the traditional snakes of the snake charmer, but they react to the swaying of his flute rather than to the sound as all snakes are deaf to all but the lowest frequencies and mainly detect vibrations transmitted though the ground. Some snake charmers also take the added precaution of periodically removing the fangs.

♂♀ Common Chameleon *Chamaeleo chamaeleon*

Though this insectivorous, tree-dwelling lizard does undergo dramatic and rapid colour changes, it is now known that these are in response to environmental or emotional factors rather than to a need for concealment, which is accomplished by its natural coloration. Such changes are controlled by its autonomic nervous system and involve the melanophore cells in its skin, which are able to redistribute the pigment granules present. Chameleons move through the bushes, very slowly stalking their prey, which they catch by rapidly shooting out their sticky tongues that are as long as they are – 25–30cm (9.9–11.8in). They have feet adapted for clinging to branches, prehensile tails and acute, independently movable eyes. In the breeding season males compete for the females and after mating the female descends to the ground to lay 20–30 eggs in a hole dug in the earth, which she then leaves to hatch. Common Chameleons live in North Africa, southern Spain and Portugal, Crete and the Canary Islands.

♂♀ Common Garter Snake *Thamnophis sirtalis*

This is the most familiar snake of North America and, unusually for a reptile, is to be found as far north as Canada up to 67°N. The non-venomous Common Garter Snake is diurnal and feeds on frogs, toads and small invertebrates in the damp locations it frequents. Those in northern latitudes hibernate, emerging in spring to mate. The female gives birth to up to 80 live young, which feed on tadpoles and earthworms. The snake's principal defence when attacked is to release a fetid discharge from its anal gland. A member of the Colubridae family, which contains 66 per cent of all extant snake species, it reaches an adult length of 45–130cm (17.7–51.2in).

♂♀ Eastern Coral Snake or Harlequin Snake *Micrurus fulvius*

As in the case of the highly venomous Eastern Coral Snake, vivid coloration often serves as a warning to would-be predators. Interestingly, another snake, the harmless Milk Snake *Lampropeltis triangulum,* closely mimics the Eastern Coral Snake's coloration for its own protection. The vital difference between them can be discerned in the order of the coloured bands and is summed up in the mnemonic folk rhyme, 'red next to yellow, dangerous fellow'. The Eastern Coral Snake is nocturnal and rarely seen. It inhabits forests and rocky hillsides near water in the south-eastern USA and Mexico. Its diet is lizards and other snakes and it grows to 1.2m (3.9ft) long. Between 6–10 eggs are laid in damp ground and hatch to reveal young about 5cm (almost 2in) long.

♂♀ Estuarine Crocodile *Crocodylus porosus*

The crocodile is a survivor from the age of the dinosaurs. It physically differs from the alligator in the way some of its teeth are visible when the jaws are closed. The Estuarine Crocodile is considered dangerous to man and lives in brackish and salt water and can sometimes even be found swimming out at sea. Its home is the estuaries, coasts and mangrove swamps of northern Australia, Indonesia and southern India and, despite controls, it is extensively hunted for its valuable hide. Estuarine Crocodiles grow to lengths of up to 8m (over 26ft), but are commonly 4–6m (roughly 13–19ft). They catch their prey by lying motionless in water with only their eyes and nostrils visible until an animal comes close. After seizing it they drag it underwater to drown before dismembering and eating it. After mating, the female lays 25–90 eggs into a crude nest made from plant debris that serves as an incubator. All crocodiles ingest stones possibly to act as ballast or aid digestion. It is not surprising that such an awesome and impressive beast as the crocodile should have been venerated in ancient Egypt as Sebek, the crocodile-headed god associated with fertility and the protector of kings, during the 13th Dynasty.

♂♀ Galapagos Giant Tortoise *Geochelone elephantopus*

The Galapagos Giant Tortoise is only found on the islands of the Galapagos archipelago. It was first studied by Charles Darwin who noted the distinct differences between races on separate islands, which ultimately led to his momentous theory of evolution set out in *On the Origin of Species . . .* (1859). The largest of these vegetarians may measure 1.5m (4.9ft) long and weigh more than 225kg (496lb); the males are considerably larger than the females. Mating takes place at any time of the year and the female lays about 24 eggs in a hole dug in soil. She leaves them to be warmed by the sun until they hatch when the young are immediately able to fend for themselves. The Galapagos Giant Tortoise can live for possibly 200 years.

Populations of this reptile are greatly reduced as in the past sailors took them as an easy source of fresh meat.

♂♀ Green Turtle *Chelonia mydas*

Green Turtles are, in fact, brownish and their name derives from their green fat evident in the famous, eponymous soup. The Green Turtle has the dubious distinction of being the most widely eaten reptile and it is now listed as an endangered species. This creature generally grows to 102–127cm (40–50in) long, but larger specimens are known. It is pelagic, rarely coming ashore except to lay eggs and bask. It feeds on seaweed and, it is believed, on some crustaceans and jellyfish. Every 2–3 years mature Green Turtles return to the place of their birth to mate. The female then hauls herself up on to the beach to dig a shallow hole into which she lays a clutch of more than 100 eggs that she subsequently buries. Like crocodiles, turtles have the extraordinary ability to determine the eventual sex of their clutch of eggs, though it is thought that this is not a conscious faculty. The temperature of the sand in which the eggs incubate determines the sex of the offspring; those that develop at a warmer temperature eventually hatch as females and those buried in cooler places become males. When the young turtles hatch, they dig their way to the surface and instinctively head for the sea, running a gauntlet of waiting predators.

♂♀ Large Toad-headed Agamid *Phrynocephalus mystaceus*

There are more than 300 species of lizard in the agamid family distributed throughout the Old World. The Large Toad-headed Agamid comes from Central Asia and Afghanistan; its coloration enables it to blend in with the desert sands where it makes its home. It often conceals itself by moving its body rapidly from side to side until it is buried in the sand. If threatened, it frequently opens its mouth, which is apparently enlarged by flaplike extensions at the corners of its jaws. This usually intimidates its attacker, which is normally a bird, snake, monitor or small carnivore. It measures about 20cm (7.8in) and spends the winter in an underground burrow emerging in April to begin mating in May–June. Two clutches of 2–6 eggs are laid each year. The diet of the Large Toad-headed Agamid is insects, their larvae and other small invertebrates.

♂♀ Spectacled Caiman *Caiman crocodilus*

The Spectacled Caiman is a 1.5–2.5m (4.9–8.2ft) long relative of the alligator and can be found in slow-moving waters and swamps between the Amazon and Orinoco basins and southern Mexico. It was imported to the USA when the native alligator population there began to decline and hunting was prohibited. Though it is the most abundant species of caiman, the Spectacled Caiman is nevertheless hunted for its skin and the young are sold as pets or as stuffed curios. After mating the female lays 30–40 eggs in a concealed nest she digs in soft earth

There are more than birds, bats and balloons
flying around here. By now the sharp-eyed will have identified
several couples in this book so far. Try to find a vociferous insect
and a bird with a loud voice, a mammal with a nose for luck,
an occasionally greedy grasshopper and a creature that feeds
on poisonous plants. Remember, not only birds lay eggs
(and don't forget the snail).

near the water. These are guarded until the young hatch. It derives its common name from the spectacle-like ridge between the eyes.

BIRDS

The approximately 9000 extant species of bird are warm-blooded, air-breathing vertebrates that are covered in feathers and reproduce by laying eggs. All birds have wings but not all are capable of flight; some species are exclusively terrestrial and others have wings that have been adapted as underwater paddles. Over 900 further species are thought to have once existed. The smallest bird is generally considered to be the Bee Hummingbird *Mellisuga helenae* from Cuba, which is only 57mm (2.2in) long and weighs less than 3g (0.1oz). The largest is the Ostrich *Struthio camelus*, which can stand as tall as 2.5m (8ft) and weigh up to 155kg (over 341lb). Even this giant is not as tall as the extinct Moa *Diornia maximus* of New Zealand, which is believed to have reached over 3m (9.8ft) and to have coexisted with early man. The earliest known bird is Archaeopteryx *Archaeopteryx lithographica*, which dates from the upper Jurassic period (160 million years ago); some consider it was possibly the link between modern birds and their reptilian ancestors, sharing characteristics with both classes. Birds are to be found almost anywhere on the planet from the abundant communities in tropical forests to the occasional wayward individual reported near the poles.

♂♀ Andean Condor *Vultur gryphus*

The solitary Andean Condor is the world's largest flying bird. It measures 130cm (51.2in), weighs 12kg (26.5lb) and has a wingspan of over 3m (9.8ft). It is a member of the family of New World vultures (Cathartidae) which, though superficially similar to the Old World vultures in appearance and feeding habits, is unrelated. The Andean Condor feeds on carrion and ranges from the high Andes to the Pacific coast of South America. It breeds bi-annually when (usually) 1 egg is laid in a lofty nest constructed on a rocky ledge at altitudes of 3000m (9843ft) or more. These eggs are incubated by both parents after which the newly hatched young are fed on regurgitated food until they can leave the nest 6 months later. Male condors have a distinctive, fleshy caruncle on their forehead.

♂♀ Arctic Tern *Sterna paradisaea*

Not counting humans aided by machines, the most travelled creature on earth is probably the Arctic Tern, which undertakes incredibly long annual migrations of up to 36,000km (22,356 miles) between the Arctic and Antarctic throughout its life. Returning to its northern breeding grounds in April–May it mates and in a shallow scraped nest usually 2 eggs are laid that are incubated by both parents. The predation rate is high with many of the eggs and fledglings taken by gulls, skuas and other predators. Fed at first by their parents, the young birds are capable of flight by 4 weeks when they can join the adults in feeding by plunge-diving in the sea for small fish and crustaceans living near the surface. Adult Arctic Terns measure 38cm (almost 15in).

♂♀ Atlantic Puffin *Fratercula arctica*

The Puffin is a member of the Auk family (Alcidae) that fills a similar ecological niche in the northern hemisphere to the penguins in the southern. In fact, the now extinct flightless Great Auk *Pinguinis impennis* was originally called the penguin and only later was this name transferred to the similar looking bird that we know today. The most striking feature of the Puffin is its brightly coloured, striped bill, which becomes smaller and duller outside the breeding season. This bird, which measures 29–36cm (11.4–14.2in), is found in the north Atlantic as far south as Maine and Brittany but it rarely comes ashore except to breed from late May. Breeding pairs make use of abandoned burrows or else dig their own and lay a single egg. Both parents incubate the egg and the resulting chick is fed by them. They are capable of carrying several small fish at a time in their capacious bills. When the chick is about 6 weeks old the parents return to sea to moult. During this period they are flightless and must escape danger by diving. A week later the chick, which is also initially flightless, emerges from its burrow, compelled by hunger to join its parents.

♂♀ Avocet *Recurvirostra avosetta*

The elegant Avocet with its distinctive, upwardly curving bill spends the summer months on its breeding grounds in Europe and western and Central Asia. The northern populations migrate each winter to West Africa and southern Asia. These long-legged birds are specialized waders that feed in the shallow waters of coastal pools, estuaries and mud flats. They search for small aquatic animals, especially crustaceans and worms (Annalida), also insects and some plant matter, which they find by sweeping their bills from side to side. Sometimes several birds will form a line to herd crustaceans or small fish. After mating a crude scrape is excavated near the water's edge into which the female lays 3–5 eggs that are incubated by both parents. The sexes are similar and an adult measures about 43cm (17in).

♂♀ Bald Eagle *Haliaeetus leucocephalus*

Since 1782 the mainly fish-eating Bald Eagle has been the emblematic bird of the USA and is distributed along coasts, rivers and lakes from Alaska to the Gulf of Mexico. Greatly persecuted in the past, the estimated 5000 surviving birds are now strictly protected by law. Bald Eagles mate for life (often 40 years) and breed from late winter–early spring when 2–3 eggs are laid in a tree nest. This nest is enlarged each season and eventually measures 3m (9.8ft) across and 4m (13.1ft) high. Both partners incubate the eggs. Bald Eagles are named for their white head plumage and an adult male measures 80cm (31.5in) and the female 110cm (43.3in) with a wingspan of up to 2.2m (7.2ft) and a weight of 6.5kg (14.3lb).

♂♀ Barn Owl *Tyto alba*

The Barn Owl is a cosmopolitan species, which is found on every continent except Antarctica. Like many owls, it is nocturnal, measures about 34cm (13.4in) and feeds mainly on small rodents such as shrews, mice and rats but it also takes small birds and reptiles. It hunts using its superb senses of hearing and sight as well as its ability to fly soundlessly, because its flight feathers are covered with a downy surface, and therefore take its prey unawares. It swallows its prey whole and the indigestible parts are later regurgitated as hard pellets that betray its roost to the keen-eyed. The Barn Owl does not build nests but uses holes in trees, rock crevices or old farm buildings in which to lay its clutch of 4–7 eggs, which are incubated by the female. The owl was associated with the Greek goddess Athena and later with her Roman counterpart Minerva who, though known as the goddess of war, was also the goddess of the arts, handicrafts and wisdom. In modern western culture the owl remains symbolic of wisdom.

♂♀ Bewick's Swan *Cygnus bewickii*

Swans are the largest flying waterfowl. Bewick's Swan is regarded as conspecific with the Whistling Swan *C. Columbianus* and is a native of the swamps and marshes of the Palaearctic region. Males (cobs) and females (pens) are similar in appearance; a large male measures 1.4m (about 4.6ft) and the female is slightly smaller. Swans generally mate for life and, contrary to popular belief, can be quite vocal – including the Mute Swan *C. olor*. Bewick's Swans breed in northern Russia and migrate south to Europe for the winter. The juveniles (cygnets) accompany their parents on this long journey. When the cygnets emerge from their clutch of 3–5 eggs, they have a mottled grey plumage and acquire their distinctive white coats only at maturity. Their principal diet is aquatic vegetation, which they collect by dabbling in shallow water.

♂♀ Black-and-yellow Broadbill *Eurylaimus ochromalus*

The chunky Black-and-yellow Broadbill, which is 16.6cm (6.5in) in length, belongs to the family Eurylaimidae and lives in the tropical forests of the Malay Peninsula, Sumatra, Borneo and other smaller islands nearby at altitudes of up to 900m (almost 3000ft). It is a relatively slow-moving bird that feeds mainly on insects as well as fruit, seeds and other plant material. Little information is available about its breeding habits but its scruffy, pendant nests are seen on branches overhanging forest streams. It lays 3 eggs. Black-and-yellow Broadbills have loud voices similar to the chirring of cicadas.

Blue Tit *Parus caeruleus*

♂♀

Agile and colourful, Blue Tits are familiar residents of parks, gardens and woodlands throughout Europe, excluding the far north of Scandinavia. They are principally insectivorous but in the winter months they also feed on seeds and nuts and are among the most frequent visitors to garden bird tables. In spring they nest in holes in trees or nest boxes, producing 5–16 eggs. The newborn chicks are continually fed by both parents until they quit the nest 15–23 days later. In the south of their range a second brood is often produced in July. Blue Tits typically measure 11.5cm (4.5in).

Blue-winged Pitta *Pitta brachyura*

♂♀

Among the most colourful of birds, Pittas are sometimes also called 'jewel thrushes'. Their long legs reflect their terrestrial feeding habits; they scratch around in leaf litter on the forest floor searching for insects and small invertebrates. The summers are passed in northern and Central India and the winters further south, including Sri Lanka. A globular nest is built in a tree where 4–6 eggs are laid and the chicks are raised and fed by both parents. When fully grown Blue-winged Pittas measure 18cm (7in).

Brown Kiwi or Common Kiwi *Apteryx australis*

♂♀

The national bird of New Zealand, the Kiwi, occurs only in this country where it is endemic. A shy, nocturnal bird, its rudimentary wings are concealed beneath its feathers that are like coarse hair and ideal for repelling the dense undergrowth where it makes its home. The Kiwi detects food by smell, using its long bill, which has nostrils near the tip, to probe among the forest litter or to thrust deep into the soil. It eats small invertebrates, seeds and berries. Its name is derived from its harsh call. After mating, 1–2 eggs are laid by the female in an underground burrow which, in comparison to her size of about 50cm (19.7in), are enormous at around 450g (15.8oz) or about one-quarter of the female's body size. These are cared for by the smaller male until they hatch to produce chicks that are fully feathered and open-eyed and do not need to eat for a week.

Brown Thrasher *Toxostoma refum*

♂♀

The Brown Thrasher is a member of the mockingbird family (Mimidae) and is widespread throughout the USA east of the Rocky Mountains. The sexes are similarly plumaged. It feeds on the ground on seeds, fruit and small invertebrates. It builds low nests and both parents share the incubation of the 4–5 eggs. The chicks are ready to leave the nest after 9–12 days. The woodland- and scrub-dwelling Brown Thrasher is 30cm (11.8in) in length.

Budgerigar *Melopsittacus undulatus*

♂♀

One of the world's most popular cage birds. The natural home of this small, brightly coloured parrot is the scrub and open country of the Australian interior where large flocks can be found searching the ground for grass seeds. They feed at dawn and in the late afternoon and flocks are constantly on the move to new feeding areas. In the wild Budgerigars are predominantly yellow and green but their coloration when captively bred varies greatly. Their average size is 18cm (7in). Budgerigars breed throughout the year and lay 4–6 eggs in hollow logs or tree stumps. The eggs are incubated by the female. The young are ready to leave the nest after 1 month.

Bullfinch *Pyrrhula pyrrhula*

♂♀

The shy, arboreal Bullfinch is widespread in Europe (except southern Spain and northern Scandinavia), Asia and Japan. It frequents parks, gardens, forests and farmland areas. At times it can be a nuisance in orchards because of the damage it causes to young buds. The female builds a nest in April and lays about 5 eggs. The chicks are fed by both parents until they are fledged at 16 days. The coloration of the sexes differs and adults grow to 14.7cm (5.8in).

Canada Goose *Branta canadensis*

♂♀

This waterfowl is exceeded in size only by the swan. It occurs all over North America and has been successfully introduced to northern Europe and New Zealand. Each autumn flocks migrate south, along the same routes used for generations, in typical 'V' formations, calling with a loud, hoarse and repeated 'honking'. There are 12 geographically distinct races of Canada Geese with corresponding variations in size from 56–110cm (22–43in). The female lays about 5 eggs, which she incubates until the young (goslings) emerge. Later they form flocks that forage at dawn and dusk for grass, grain, seeds and berries.

Cedar Waxwing *Bombycilla cedrorum*

♂♀

The Waxwings derive their common name from the shiny red, wax-like beads on the tips of their secondary wing feathers. These are actually elongations of the feather shaft. Cedar Waxwings are found in Canada and the USA and inhabit coniferous and open deciduous woodlands. In winter they sometimes invade gardens and parks to eat berries, which is their preferred diet. A loose, bulky nest is constructed and 3–6 eggs are laid and tended by the female. Adults measure about 16–17cm (6.3–6.7in).

Cockatiel *Nymphicus hollandicus*

♂♀

Cockatiels have slender crests on their head. Popular cage birds, their natural habitat is the open country and grasslands of the Australian interior where small flocks feed on the seeds of grasses, shrubs or trees and on grains, small fruits and berries. The breeding season is normally between August–December and soon after mating 4–7 eggs are laid and incubated by both parents. Cockatiels measure 32cm (12.6in) and their adult coloration is brighter in the male than the female.

Collared Pratincole *Glareola pratincola*

♂♀

Collared Pratincoles are conspicuous in flight because of their elegant shape, narrow, pointed wings and deeply forked tails. On the ground these gregarious birds are able runners but they also like to feed high in the air, chasing flying insects. They breed on open plains in loose colonies; 2–4 camouflaged eggs are laid on the ground and incubated by both parents. Collared Pratincoles are summer visitors that breed from southern Europe to Central Asia. They migrate south after breeding to sub-equatorial Africa. They are sometimes also known as Swallow Plovers and typically measure 25cm (nearly 10in). They are usually found on plains, marshes and sun-baked mud flats near water.

Collared Puffbird *Bucco capensis*

♂♀

Puffbirds are related to jacamars and are distributed throughout the lowlands of northern South America east of the Andes. They feed on flying insects, which they catch in flight after launching themselves from a perch, as well as occasionally on small frogs and lizards. They nest in chambers at the end of long holes excavated by both parents that also share in the care of the 2–3 eggs. The sexes are similar in appearance and measure 18cm (7.1in). They get their common name from their habit of puffing out their feathers when perched.

Common Cassowary or Double-wattled Cassowary *Casuarius casuarius*

♂♀

Notwithstanding the artistic licence employed in this picture, the Cassowary is among the largest of birds, third only in size to the Ostrich and the Emu. Females are larger than males and measure 1.8m (5.9ft) high. Cassowaries are flightless, having only vestigial wings, and live in the Australasian rainforests. They have powerful legs and the innermost toe of each foot bears a sharp, dagger-like nail, which can inflict a severe wound and has even been known to kill a man. After the female has laid 3–6 eggs, the male incubates them in a nest scrape on the ground, which is lined with leaves. The young have a brown plumage with longitudinal stripes that vanish to become a uniform brown in adolescence and black in maturity. The chief diet of Cassowaries is fruit and small animals.

Common Redpoll *Acanthis flammea*

♂♀

This small finch has a bright crimson forehead, which gives it its common name. It is one of the most northern of the songbirds and is distributed from Iceland, the British Isles and

Here's a couple of igneous amphibians.
Maybe there are more and maybe not, but don't shed crocodile tears
if things seem a little clouded. The flags are out for a prickly
customer and a bellicose fish – among others. There's a dog
that's been painted in more ways than one, a religious insect,
an imperial one too and a lunar rodent.
Did I remember to include the snail?

throughout northern Europe east to the Bering Sea. It is also found in northern America and its length is 13–15cm (5.1–5.9in). It feeds on alder and birch seeds and also, in summer, on small insects. Typically, the nest is built in a silver birch and placed in a fork 2–3m (6.6–9.8ft) high. The female lays 4–6 eggs, which she incubates alone.

♂♀ Common Turkey *Meleagris gallopavo*

The Common Turkey was originally introduced to Europe in the sixteenth century by the Spanish, who brought specimens back from the New World where it was at one time a sacred bird. Most turkeys are domesticated and much larger than native birds, but in the wild they grow to 91–122cm (about 36–48in) and weigh up to 10kg (22lb). The males (called toms or gobblers) are larger than the females (hens) and each year in February they gather together a harem with which to breed. Nesting begins in April and the hen lays 8–15 eggs, which she incubates until the young (poults) hatch. At the end of the mating season the males are emaciated from fighting rival males and impregnating females. The wild Common Turkey lives in light woodland and eats seeds, nuts, berries and small invertebrates and is a strong flyer over distances up to 0.5km (0.3 mile).

♂♀ Cormorant *Phalacrocorax carbo*

Also known as Great or Black Cormorants, these are fish-eating water birds that are about 94cm (37in) in length and inhabit lakes, marshes and sea coasts of Eurasia, North America, Africa and Australia. In the Orient some are caught and trained to catch fish using their natural fishing method of diving underwater for 20–30 seconds at a time. Their wings are clipped and their throats constricted just below their gular sac or throat pouch to prevent them swallowing their catch, which is disgorged by the fishermen when the birds surface. Breeding colonies vary in size but some can reach several thousand pairs. Breeding takes place in the spring. Cormorants build nests in trees or on rocky ledges where 3–5 eggs are laid and cared for by both parents.

♂♀ Corncrake *Crex crex*

This secretive member of the rail family (Rallidae) is well camouflaged and, because it lives in luxuriant grassy meadows, it can be difficult to see, though its harsh grating call is very obvious. It is 26.5cm (10.4in) in length. After breeding in Europe and Asia, it migrates south to tropical Africa to overwinter, arriving back at its breeding grounds in May. Following mating the female lays anything from 6–18 mottled eggs in a well-concealed nest on the ground among long grass or nettles. The eggs are cared for by the female. The chicks are born black and only acquire their adult coloration later. Corncrakes feed on seeds, grain, insects and worms.

♂♀ Cuckoo *Cuculus canorus*

The Cuckoo is named after the distinctive call of the male, which is the traditional herald of spring. Outside the mating season Cuckoos are solitary birds frequenting woodlands and moors where they feed on large insects, with a particular preference for hairy caterpillars, which are unpalatable to most other birds. Cuckoos are infamous as brood-parasitic birds; the female lays a single egg in 8–12 different nests on alternate days, ejecting one of the host birds' own eggs to do so. When the egg, which often, but by no means always, resembles those of the host, hatches, the parasite chick, which is much bigger and more powerful than its hosts' young, throws them out and receives all the adults' subsequent care. It soon grows far larger than its 'parents' and eventually reaches a length of 33cm (13in). The Cuckoo is distributed throughout Europe, North Africa and large parts of Asia. It migrates in July–September to the south of its range to overwinter.

♂♀ Domestic Chicken *Gallus gallus*

Although some authorities like to name the modern Domestic Chicken *G. domesticus*, it is identical to its wild ancestor, the Red Jungle Fowl *G. gallus* of south-eastern Asia. It is known that Chickens were domesticated in China as long ago as the second millennium BC and that by 300 BC they had been brought to the Mediterranean countries, arriving in western Europe about 200 years later. Domestic Chickens are usually categorized into 4 groups: layers; table; dual-purpose; and fancy. Layers are bred for egg production and include such breeds as the Leghorn and Welsummer. Table birds bred for their flesh include the Dorking and Faverolle while dual-purpose breeds, such as the Rhode Island Red and Orpington, are the most common and combine the qualities of both the layers and table birds. The fancy breeds include the bantams, fighting birds and those kept for their appearance like the remarkable Long-tailed Yokohama, which has tail feathers that reach lengths of over 6m (19.7ft). In ancient Rome soothsayers used Chickens in the *oraculum ex tripudio*, in which the omens were decided by the amount the birds ate. The cock or male Chicken is the emblematic bird of France.

♂♀ Eclectus Parrot *Eclectus roratus*

This noisy and conspicuous bird is found in north-eastern Queensland, where it is known as the Rocky River Parrot, and is also distributed in the Sunda and Solomon Islands and New Guinea. An inhabitant of tropical forests, the most distinctive feature of the Eclectus Parrot is its pronounced sexual dimorphism and for many years males and females were believed to be separate species. Flocks of up to 80 birds feed on fruit, seeds, nuts, berries and nectar. Insects are also taken and these parrots grow to about 35cm (13.8in). They form pairs in the breeding season and 2 eggs are laid and incubated by the female for 26 days in a nest perched in a tree trunk. The young

are subsequently cared for by both parents until they leave the nest at 10–12 weeks.

♂♀ Emu *Dromaius novaehollandiae*

The flightless Emu, the second largest living bird, stands about 2m (6.6ft) tall, and is the sole member of the Dromaiidae family. Today it is found on the Australian mainland only. The females weigh as much as 45kg (99.2lb) while the smaller males might weigh 36kg (79.4lb). Emus' principal food is seeds, fruit, flowers, grass and insects and they commonly ingest stones as large as 2.5cm (1in) in diameter into the gizzard to aid grinding this diet. Emus are monogamous and breed during the winter (May–August in the southern hemisphere). After the female has laid 9–12 eggs in an untidy nest on the ground, the male incubates them. The eggs are incubated at only 35°C (91.4°F) and during this period the male does not eat or drink. Once hatched, the chicks, which initially are cream-coloured with longitudinal stripes, leave the nest after only 48 hours.

♂♀ European Bee-eater *Merops apiaster*

As might be deduced from their common name, these gaudy birds could be unpopular with apiarists but their diet also includes other hymenopterous insects such as wasps whose venomous stings are discharged against their perch before they are eaten. The Bee-eaters arrive in the warmer regions of Europe, North Africa and south-western Asia from their African winter quarters in April–May to breed in colonies. A 1.2–3m (3.9–9.8ft) burrow is dug in a sandy bank where 4–7 eggs are laid. These are incubated and the chicks cared for by both parents. European Bee-eaters are about 28cm (11in) long.

♂♀ European Goldfinch *Carduelis carduelis*

Although commonly called the European Goldfinch, this attractive member of the finch family (Fringillidae) can also be found in North Africa, the mid-Atlantic islands, Central and southern Asia as far as the Himalayas. It has been introduced into Australasia, the USA and Bermuda and other places. Males and females are similar and typically measure 12cm (4.7in). Their main diet is the seeds of weeds, especially those of the thistle and teasel. The female builds the nest in a tree and lays 3–7 eggs that she incubates while the male feeds her. The collective noun for a group of these birds is a 'charm' of Goldfinches.

♂♀ European Nuthatch *Sitta europaea*

Largely insectivorous in the summer months, in the winter ones the Nuthatch also eats seeds and nuts that it wedges in tree bark and cracks open with its bill. Worldwide there are about 25 species, of which the majority occur in Eurasia. The home of *S. europaea* is western Europe, except for northern Scandinavia and Ireland, where it can be seen in parks, gardens and open woodland. Nuthatches are agile climbers and can easily work their way up or down tree trunks or branches in quest of insects or larvae. In spring the female lays 4–13 eggs in a hole in a tree and incubates alone. Adult Nuthatches are 14cm (5.5in) in length.

European Swallow or Barn Swallow
Hirundo rustica

In Europe the graceful Swallow is considered the harbinger of spring when it arrives in early April from its winter quarters in sub-equatorial Africa. This species occurs worldwide but breeds in the northern hemisphere between latitudes 30°N and 70°N. Once an inhabitant of cliffs and crags, this bird now finds more agreeable dwelling places close to human habitation; its open nests made from straw glued together with mud are often to be found on the rafters of old barns and in disused buildings. The female, which is distinguished from the male only by her slightly duller plumage and slightly shorter tail, typically lays a clutch of 5 eggs and may produce a second brood. The Swallow feeds on airborne insects that it catches while in its wonderfully agile flight. An average European Swallow measures 19.5cm (7.7in). Each autumn it forms large flocks before heading south.

Firecrest *Regulus ignicapillus*

The Firecrest is a minute 9cm (about 3.5in) member of the family of Warblers (Sylviidae) and it makes its home in coniferous and mixed woodland. It gets its name from its vividly coloured crest and is distributed throughout Europe south of Scandinavia. In the winter this range is reduced to southern France, Spain, Portugal, Italy and Greece. Firecrests nest in spring and build suspended nests in a fir tree. They lay 4–7 eggs. When these hatch they are cared for by both parents.

Fulmar *Fulmarus glacialis*

The Fulmar is a large, robust member of the petrel family and is well known to commercial fishing fleets in northern waters as a scavenger of discarded fish waste. Due to the increase of this industry, it is vastly more numerous today than in bygone years. It is an expert swimmer and a spectacular flyer, but seldom dives and then only to very shallow depths. Fulmars spend most of their lives on the high seas and from early spring collect in huge offshore 'rafts' before breeding on cliffs or rocky islands in May or June. Breeding takes place often in colonies of thousands of birds and after the female has laid a single egg it is incubated in turns by both parents. Fulmars defend their chick by the disagreeable method of spitting a foul-smelling stomach oil at would-be predators. Both sexes are similar in appearance and typically measure 45–50cm (17.7–19.7in) long.

Golden Eagle *Aquila chrysaetos*

The majestic Golden Eagle is the world's most widely distributed large eagle occupying mountainous areas throughout most of the Holarctic region as far south as Mexico and North Africa. These large birds of prey reach 89cm (35in) and have wingspans of 188–230cm (74–90in). They are equipped with powerful talons for seizing rabbits, hares and ptarmigan. In March–April a nest (eyrie) is built on an inaccessible cliff or sometimes in a tree where (usually) 2 eggs are laid and incubated by the female while she is fed by the male. The first chick (eaglet) to hatch often kills its sibling, especially if there is a shortage of prey that year. The Golden Eagle is the emblematic bird of Mexico and appears on its flag grasping a snake.

Goosander *Mergus merganser*

Sexually dimorphic, the 57.5cm (22.6in) female Goosander has a crested head, unlike the larger 75.5cm (29.7in) male. The range of this duck extends throughout the Holarctic region. The species is migratory in the far north of its range. From March–May 7–16 eggs are typically laid in a nest in a hollow tree and incubated by the female. Soon after the young hatch they are encouraged to leap from their lofty nest to the water below, where they join their mother. The adults take a variety of small fish, both freshwater and coastal, and also crustaceans, insects and larvae.

Greater Flamingo *Phoenicopterus ruber*

The Greater Flamingo is the largest of the 5 species of this most colourful of the social wading birds. It feeds by wading in shallow, brackish water where it finds small molluscs, crustaceans and other organic matter, which is then sieved just beneath the surface by its lamellated bill held upside down. Flamingos breed often irregularly in colonies numbering thousands of birds along the sub-tropical Atlantic and Gulf coasts of America and on the lagoons of the Mediterranean coasts of France and Spain. They also breed on other widely scattered saline lakes from Africa to Central Asia. A nest is made in the form of a truncated cone of mud and the female lays 1–2 eggs, which are incubated by both parents. Males and females are similar in size and appearance and measure about 114cm (44.9in). Flamingo tongues were considered a great delicacy by the Romans.

Great Indian Hornbill *Buceros bicornis*

The home of the Great Indian Hornbill is the forests of India, south-east Asia and Sumatra; it can be found at elevations up to 2000m (6562ft). The chief feature of these large birds, which reach 1.5m (4.9ft), is their massive bill and 'casque' which is quite light as it is made from a honeycomb of bony, cellular tissue with a hard, horny casing. It feeds chiefly on wild figs and other fruits and occasionally takes small lizards, rats and nesting birds. After mating the female lays 1–3 eggs in a hole in a tree and while still inside walls up the entrance with her own faeces and mud, leaves and figs brought by the male. This hardens like concrete. Here she incubates the eggs while the male feeds her through a tiny slit. During the time she is immured she keeps the nest clean having evolved the ability to defecate at high velocity through the feeding slit. When the chicks hatch they remain safely inside with their mother. After about 14 days she breaks out and the young reclose the entrance to be fed by both their parents through the same slit until they are fully fledged and can leave the nest.

Great Kiskadee *Pitangus sulphuratus*

The Kiskadee gets its name from its loud 'kis-ka-dee' call and is a familiar bird throughout most of its range from south-eastern Texas to Argentina. It uses a conspicuous perch and launches out into the air for small beetles, wasps and other flying insects. It also takes small lizards and fish when it behaves like a kingfisher by plunging into the water from its perch. It takes some berries and fruit when other food is scarce. Kiskadees measure 23–26cm (9–10in) and make large, oval nests high in a tree where the female usually lays 4 eggs.

Great Skua or Bonxie *Catharacta skua*

Normally solitary and pelagic, Great Skuas form loose colonies in the breeding season. They breed mainly in Iceland, the Faroes, the Shetland and Orkney Islands and occasionally in mainland Scotland. Two eggs are produced and incubated by both sexes. The chicks are fed on regurgitated food by both parents. They chase other seabirds and force them to drop or disgorge fish. They also eat the eggs and young of other species of seabird as well as carrion. Great Skuas grow to 51–60cm (20–23.6in); the females are slightly larger than the males. At the end of the breeding season, Great Skuas move south into the Atlantic to winter off the coasts of North Africa and Brazil.

Great White Egret *Egretta alba*

Although absent from most of Europe, this graceful heron is otherwise distributed virtually throughout the rest of the world where it inhabits the margins of shallow water. The Great White Egret grows to 90–120cm (35.5–47.3in). In the breeding season its bill – in most populations – becomes black and it develops striking nuptial plumes on its back that are highly prized as ceremonial and fashion accessories. Between 2–5 eggs are laid in a nest made in a reed bed or tree and incubated in turn by both parents. The bird catches its prey by either stalking or waiting motionless to grasp fish, insects or small mammals in its long, sharp beak.

Green Woodpecker *Picus viridis*

Green Woodpeckers are residents in Europe and southern Scandinavia, Turkey, Iran, western Russia and North Africa and are found in deciduous woodland, parks, orchards and gardens. They feed on ants and on the larvae of xylophagous beetles, which they find by their typical pecking at tree bark. Breeding takes place in April–May and a pair drill out a nesting cavity in a tree about 50cm (19.7in) deep and 5m (16.4ft) or more from the ground. A second hole nearby may be used for sleeping; both nests are used for several successive years. Some 4–7 eggs are

Here's a third pair of animals plus some mates
for creatures you have encountered before in this book.
There are also some new animals, one of which might pander to
your lesser whims. Try to find a tempestuous seabird,
a talkative antipodean, a pisciform toxophilite and a xylophonic dove.
By now you should have found a dozen (or more) couples
and four snails.

laid and incubated by the male and female. Fully grown Green Woodpeckers are about 32cm (12.6in) long.

♂♀ Grey Butcher-bird *Cracticus torquatus*

Butcher-birds are so named for their habit of impaling or otherwise wedging their prey – which can be a small vertebrate or large insect – on a thorn or cleft branch in order to dismember and eat it. Grey Butcher-birds live in Australia in open woodland, eucalypt forests and on the margins of rainforests. They are typically 24–30cm (9.5–11.8in). At breeding time couples perform impressively melodic duets and 3–5 eggs are laid in an untidy saucer-shaped tree nest, which is vigorously defended even against humans.

♂♀ Grey Heron *Ardea cinerea*

The Grey Heron is a native of Europe, Africa and Asia where it can be found in, or near, shallow water. It stands motionless on its long legs for extended periods until its prey – usually fish, eels and frogs – comes within range whereupon it darts its long neck forward and grasps its meal with its slender bill. This bill is rich in mucus, which sticks to its plumage. To counter this it has evolved friable powder-down feathers on its breast that produce an amorphous powder with which it preens itself. These birds breed in colonies in trees where they produce 3–5 young which are cared for by both parents. The sexes are similar and a typical Grey Heron measures 92cm (36in).

♂♀ Hammerhead or Hammerkop
Scopus umbretta

This crepuscular wading bird is also known as the Anvil-head or Hammer-headed Stork for its distinctive profile. It is the sole member of the family Scopidae. The Hammerhead is distributed from south-western Arabia through tropical Africa to Madagascar and is considered a bird of ill omen by many tribes. Found in areas of swamp, marshes and slow-moving streams, it feeds on small fish, molluscs, frogs and aquatic insects and it sometimes uses the backs of hippopotamuses as observation platforms. In the breeding season it builds a gigantic domed nest of sticks up to 1.8m (5.9ft) in diameter and 1.2m (3.9ft) high where 3–6 eggs are laid. The chicks are cared for by both parents and are ready to leave the nest after 7–8 weeks. Hammerheads grow to 50–60cm (19.7–23.6in).

♂♀ Herring Gull *Larus argentatus*

Herring Gulls are great opportunists. Originally, they were coastal birds feeding on molluscs, crabs and fish or pillaging the nests of other seabirds for eggs and fledglings but today they are scavengers *par excellence* often found far inland especially where man has created easy food sources such as refuse dumps and tips. They accompany fishing boats at sea or in harbour and, because of these additional food sources, have greatly increased in number and extended their range in recent times. Herring

Gulls are to be found over most of the northern hemisphere and the sexes are similar; they measure 55–65cm (21.8–25.6in). The chicks are hatched from a clutch of 2–3 eggs, which are incubated by both their parents.

♂♀ Hoatzin *Opisthocomus hoazin*

The Hoatzin is a curious, unique bird that lives among waterside trees in the tropical rainforests of South America. A mature specimen measures 65cm (25.6in), but weighs no more than 1kg (2.2lb). Its diet consists of leaves, flowers and fruits from marsh plants and riverside trees. A stick and twig nest is built in trees or bushes overhanging water. The female lays 2–5 eggs. After hatching, the chicks, which are capable of swimming, sometimes drop down into the water to escape predators. When young they have small, claw-like hooks at the bend of each wing, which enable them to climb about in trees but they lose these after about 3 weeks. Hoatzins clamber about in riverside vegetation and are poor flyers, only gliding or flying short distances.

♂♀ Hoopoe *Upupa epops*

Hoopoes winter in Africa and southern Asia but arrive in their northern breeding areas, including continental Europe south of Scandinavia, each April. They inhabit open country where they walk or run about on the ground, searching for various insects, worms and other invertebrates, using their long, curved, slender bills. In May or June the female lays 5–8 eggs in a hole in a tree or wall that she incubates alone while being fed by her mate. The adult Hoopoe, which measures 28cm (11in), is easily identified by its large erectile crest, curved bill and contrastingly patterned plumage. It is mentioned in classical Greek literature and was used as a hieroglyph by the ancient Egyptians.

♂♀ Jabiru *Jabiru mycteria*

This large stork – one of only 3 present in America – is distributed from Mexico to Argentina and reaches a length of 140cm (about 55in). It is a tropical wading bird and resident near swamps, lakes and rivers where it searches for its prey, usually fish, molluscs, crustaceans, snakes and lizards. A large stick nest is built in a tree or on a ledge near water and 2–4 eggs are laid and incubated by both parents.

♂♀ Jamaican Tody *Todus todus*

The five species of Tody are all found in the larger islands of the Greater Antilles and are similar in appearance and habits. The Jamaican Tody is about 10.7cm (4.2in) and nests in earth banks where it excavates a 30cm (11.8in) long burrow with an entrance only just big enough for it. This leads to a larger nesting chamber at the end where the female lays 3–4 eggs. Jamaican Todies are fiercely territorial and mostly hunt flying insects, which they catch with an audible snap of the bill close to the ground.

♂♀ Killdeer *Charadrius vociferus*

These North American plovers have loud, piercing calls – 'kill-deer' – and are to be found frequenting fields, pastures and mud flats throughout North America and northern South America. They fill a similar ecological niche in the New World to that occupied by the European lapwing. Killdeers feed on insects and small invertebrates and typically reach 25cm (9.6in) in length. In spring the male makes a number of small scrapes on the ground, one of which is selected by the female. She lays 4 eggs, which are incubated in turn by both parents.

♂♀ Kingfisher *Alcedo atthis*

As its name suggests, the chief diet of this bird is small fish, which it catches after spotting its prey from a perch and diving into the stream or river. It grasps, rather than spears, the fish before quickly regaining the surface. Returning to its perch, it kills its catch by beating it against the branch. Sometimes it hovers before diving. Kingfishers measure about 16cm (6.3in) and are mainly non-migratory, ranging from Eurasia and North Africa to New Guinea and the Solomon Islands. Northern birds move south in severe cold spells. In the breeding season they pair and build a burrow in a river bank that has a narrow entrance and a long tunnel leading to a spherical nesting chamber where 4–8 eggs are laid. More than 1 brood may be raised in a good year. The young are fed by both parents.

♂♀ King Penguin *Aptenodytes patagonica*

King Penguins, like the other 18 species in the Penguin family, Spheniscidae, are flightless. To suit their marine existence, their wings have been adapted as underwater paddles, which they use to propel them in pursuit of their prey, which consists of crustaceans, squid and small fish, while their webbed feet act as rudders. When parties are travelling fast, they momentarily leap from the surface in what is known as 'porpoising'. On land their short, sturdy legs allow them to waddle safely on ice and snow but they can also slide on their stomachs (toboggan). King Penguins breed in November–December. The female lays a single egg. Both sexes incubate, balancing the egg on their feet, covering it with a fold of feathers. Penguins are exclusive to the southern hemisphere and most breed on Antarctica and sub-Antarctic islands. Several species occur in temperate and tropical areas with a single species – the Galapagos Penguin *Spheniscus mendiculus* – actually occurring at the equator. At 1.1m (3.6ft) the King Penguin is the second largest Penguin, slightly smaller than the Emperor Penguin *A. forsteri* at 1.2m (nearly 4ft).

♂♀ King Vulture *Sarcoramphus papa*

The mute King Vulture is a member of the New World vulture family – Cathartidae – which includes the Condor and is unrelated to the Old World vultures. To the Mayan civilization that flourished in Central America before the Spanish conquest,

Cib, the thirteenth day of the month, was represented by a hieroglyph of the King Vulture. Although it sometimes takes live creatures such as lizards, the main food source of this bird is carrion, which it is believed it locates by smell. King Vultures, which are up to 85cm (33.5in) in length, with wingspans of 2m (6.6ft), take precedence over other vultures at a carcass. They also have excellent sight and inhabit the tropical forests and savannas of Central and South America. They breed only in alternate years when a single egg is laid. The young in their first plumage are initially black and only acquire their adult coloration after 2 years.

♂♀ Lapwing or Peewit *Vanellus vanellus*

During the breeding season the Lapwing is found on farmland, marshes and wet grasslands extending from northern Europe to eastern Asia and Siberia. In late summer, flocks form and gradually move south or south-west to winter in areas that are generally frost free. The Lapwing is named 'pee-wit' after its call and this is emphasized during the males' acrobatic displays performed over the breeding territory in spring. In the breeding season – March–May – the male attempts to entice a prospective mate by scraping a token nest in the ground, which is completed by the female if he is accepted. Between 3–5 eggs are then laid and incubated by both parents. Soon after hatching the chicks leave the nest and learn to find insect food for themselves while the parents keep a watchful eye out for any crows or other predators that might take them. Lapwings feed on insects, grubs, spiders and molluscs. Their length is 32cm (12.6in).

♂♀ Long-bearded Honeyeater
Melidectes princeps

The principal diet of Honeyeaters is the nectar from flowers and they have evolved a specialized long, protrusile brush-tongue to lick it up. There are 170 species of Honeyeater worldwide that are almost exclusively confined to Australia and the south-west Pacific. Long-bearded Honeyeaters come from New Guinea where they inhabit the highest mountainous forests and scattered clumps of brush in alpine meadows. They grow to 26.5cm (10.4in). Little breeding information is available, but a single egg is laid in a loose nest built in a tree 1m (3.3ft) or more from the ground.

♂♀ Long-tailed Manakin *Chiroxiphia linearis*

In this species the sexual dimorphism is marked with the drab females contrasted against the brilliantly coloured and showy plumage of the males, which is used in courtship display. The Manakin's body size is only about 10cm (3.9in) but to this must be added the male's extravagant tail feathers that double his length. Long-tailed Manakins inhabit the mangrove swamps and forests up to 1500m (4921ft) of Central America from Mexico to Costa Rica where they feed on small fruit and various insects. Males compete for the attention of females with

intricate nuptial displays for several weeks in April–May and after mating the female is left to build a bowl-like pendant nest in which she lays 2 eggs. She cares for these alone until they hatch.

♂♀ Magnificent Frigate-bird or Man-o'-War Bird
Fregata magnificens

Magnificent Frigate-birds are superb flyers with huge wingspans of 215–245cm (84.7–96.5in) and body lengths of 95–110cm (37.4–43.3in); they often soar above the ocean for hours on end, covering vast distances and landing only to sleep or nest. They occur throughout the tropics of the Atlantic and Pacific Oceans. Frigate-birds feed in flight either scooping the surface of the sea to catch fish, squid and crustaceans or, more usually, harassing other birds into dropping their catch which they then seize in mid-air. In the breeding season the males display by inflating their splendid scarlet throat sacs, which also act as resonating chambers for their mating sounds. A flimsy stick nest is constructed in a tree and a single egg is incubated in turns by both parents.

♂♀ Magpie or Black-billed Magpie *Pica pica*

In Europe this conspicuous bird has always been regarded as an omen of bad fortune and the vestiges of this ancient superstition can be discerned today in the children's rhyme that begins 'One for sorrow, two for joy . . .' and goes on to enumerate a flock of Magpies. Magpies are resident birds with a wide distribution from Europe, North Africa, parts of Asia and western North America where they inhabit light woodland margins and open country. They are omnivorous and breed in April. They build domed nests of sticks and twigs in a tree, laying 5–10 eggs, which are incubated by the female. Magpies reach 44–57cm (17.3–22.5in) when adult and are notorious for their habit of collecting shiny objects, as immortalized in Rossini's opera *La Gazza Ladra* (The Thieving Magpie). Together with their cousins, the crows and jays, they are perhaps some of the most intelligent and highly evolved of birds.

♂♀ Mallard *Anas platyrhynchos*

Members of the duck family are to be found throughout the world except in Antarctica and a few isolated islands. Mallards in particular are found throughout the northern hemisphere almost anywhere near water and they are the ancestors of the various breeds of the familiar domestic duck with the exception of the Muscovy Duck *Cairina moschata*. They feed by dabbling on the surface for plant material and small organisms. They also reach small, bottom-dwelling creatures that they find in shallow water by submerging their heads. Like most ducks, Mallards are sexually dimorphic with the male's (drake's) breeding plumage being markedly more colourful than that of the female, but during the summer months the males undergo a period of 'eclipse' when they moult and assume a plumage similar to that

of the female. After mating, the female selects a nest site and lays 8–14 eggs that she incubates alone. An adult measures between 44–48cm (17–19in).

♂♀ Masked Lovebird *Agapornis personata*

Masked Lovebirds are attractive and popular cage birds and derive their name from the way pairs sit closely together. In the wild flocks of these small parrots (their length is about 14.5cm [5.7in]) feed mainly on seeds and berries in the woodlands and scrublands of Tanzania and Kenya, at altitudes of 1100–1700m (3609–5577ft). Masked Lovebirds nest in the hollows of trees, carrying the nesting material in their bills. Some 4–6 eggs are laid and the young are capable of flight after 44 days.

♂♀ Masked Shrike *Lanius nubicus*

The Masked Shrike, like other members of the carnivorous shrike family, has the curious habit of storing its food by impaling it on thorns in so-called 'larders'. It perches inconspicuously on a dead branch or post and flies down to catch its prey, which mainly consists of insects and small lizards. The sexes are similar and measure about 17cm (about 6.7in). The species is found in the olive groves and lightly wooded countryside of Turkey, Greece and Yugoslavia during the summer months.

♂♀ Monk Parakeet *Myiopsitta monachus*

The Monk Parakeet lives in open woodland and cultivated areas of Bolivia, Paraguay, Argentina and extreme southern Brazil. Large flocks feed on fruit, nuts, berries and shoots and cause much damage by raiding crops. The birds are most remarkable, however, for their nesting habits. When the nesting season begins in October–November they form colonies of 50–70 pairs and build huge communal nests that sometimes weigh as much as 200kg (441lb) and have been known to break the branch they are built on. When the nest is being constructed, the birds, which measure about 29cm (11.4in), are sometimes seen carrying thin sticks up to 2.5m (8.2ft) long. Within this giant nest each breeding pair has its own compartment and entrance. Up to 8 nests might be built in a single tree with other similar colonies in neighbouring trees. The female lays 5–8 eggs that are cared for by both parents.

♂♀ Needle-tailed Swift *Hirundapus caudacutus*

Among the swiftest creatures on earth, the Needle-tailed Swift can reportedly achieve speeds in excess of 160km/h (almost 100mph). Although it bears a superficial resemblance to the swallow, it is unrelated and belongs rather to the large order Apodiformes, which also includes the hummingbirds. Swifts are airborne all their lives except when resting. They travel several hundred kilometres a day. They even mate on the wing. A saucer-shaped nest made from twigs and feathers glued together with hardened saliva is built attached to a cave wall or

Let me introduce you to the swiftest creature in the world –
but perhaps you've already met? Another couple or two and some
individuals you may also have met before in this book.
Perhaps you might find a supportive serpent, a flying hieroglyph,
a fish masquerading as a mammal, a national emblem and another
loquacious Australian. There's one more snail.

inside a hollow tree and 2–3 eggs are laid. Needle-tailed Swifts breed from western Siberia to the Himalayas and east to Japan. They migrate to eastern and south-eastern Australia, arriving in mid-October to depart again in mid-April. This bird is 19–21.5cm (7.5–8.5in) in length with a long wingspan of 40cm (15.5in).

♂♀ **Northern Gannet** *Sula bassana*

This is the largest seabird to be found in the northern Atlantic. Adults reach 87–100cm (34.3–39.4in) and breed from April–June in colonies numbering many thousands in north-eastern Europe, Iceland, Greenland and Canada. They winter south to the west coasts of Africa and the Gulf of Mexico. Gannets are expert flyers and superb divers and will plunge 30m (98.4ft) or more into the sea to catch fish. Within the nesting colony the birds' nests are packed very close together. The female lays a single egg that is incubated by both parents until a chick with a ravenous appetite is hatched. By the age of 11 weeks the chick weighs 1kg (2.2lb) more than an adult.

♂♀ **Northern Screamer** *Chauna chavaria*

The Northern Screamer has the most restricted range of the 3 species of this South American waterfowl and is found only in northern Colombia and western Venezuela. It feeds on vegetation and inhabits wet grassland and marshes. Screamers are named for their raucous territorial call. They have long toes that enable them to walk on floating vegetation. Screamers pair for life and build a nest near water where 2–6 eggs are laid at 2-day intervals and are incubated by both sexes. The chick is fully grown at 3½ months and reaches a length of 71–91cm (28–35.9in).

♂♀ **Ostrich** *Struthio camelus*

The Ostrich is the largest living bird and can stand 2.8m (9ft) tall – half of which is its neck – and weigh up to 155kg (341.8lb). The slightly smaller females (hens) are brown but the males (cocks) are black with the conspicuous white wing and tail plumes. Before the First World War demand for these plumes led to the establishment of Ostrich farms but today they are farmed principally for their valuable, fine-grained skin. In the wild flocks, numbering 5–50 individuals, of this flightless bird evade predators by running at speeds of up to 70km/h (43.5mph) on their strong, 2-toed legs, leaping up to 4m (over 13ft) at a time. In the breeding season, which can be at any time of the year, a male collects a harem of 3–5 hens that lay a total of 20–30 eggs into a communal nest scraped in the ground. These eggs measure about 15 × 13cm (5.9 × 5.1in) and weigh up to 1.5kg (3.3lb) and are so large that it would take 40 hens' eggs to make an equivalent-sized omelette. The eggs are incubated mainly by the male, and the chicks are independent from birth. Ostriches live in savanna and semi-desert country and, though omnivorous, eat mostly plant food. To the disappointment of cartoonists everywhere there is no record of Ostriches burying their heads.

♂♀ **Oystercatcher** *Haematopus ostralegus*

Flocks of these large 46cm (18.1in) waders live on the coasts and estuaries of Europe and parts of Asia and Africa where they feed on crustaceans and molluscs including, of course, oysters. A nest is scraped in the ground and lined and the female lays 2–4 eggs, which both parents take turns at incubating. Oystercatchers are noisy and are sometimes also known as 'Sea-pies'.

♂♀ **Peregrine Falcon** *Falco peregrinus*

The Peregrine is justly famed for the precision and swiftness of its flight and for the extraordinary speed of its near-vertical dive (stoop) on to its prey. Understandably, the prey – a pigeon, waterfowl or other bird – is instantly stunned or killed by such an impact. Some 17 races are recognized of this virtually cosmopolitan species. It can be found in mountainous country, near sea cliffs and, in recent years, also nesting in cities, taking advantage of the large numbers of pigeons that congregate there. The 2–6 eggs are laid on a ledge and cared for mainly by the female until they hatch. A protected species, the Peregrine's length is 38–51cm (about 15–20in). They have been admired by man since time immemorial and in ancient Egypt many gods were depicted as falcon-headed. Ra, the god of the sun and of creation, had the head of a falcon as did Horus, the god of the sky.

♂♀ **Plate-billed Mountain Toucan**
Andigena laminirostris

This bird, like the other 35 species of Toucan, lives in the tropical rainforests of South America. It can be found at altitudes of between 1000–3000m (3281–9843ft) in the Andes and measures about 43cm (16.9in) when adult. In common with all Toucans, it has a large, brightly coloured bill, which, though strong, is extremely light as it is composed of a bony, honeycomb material. The bill, which is used for feeding on various fruits, is also used in courtship and territorial display. These gregarious birds use old woodpecker or natural holes in trees as nests in which 2–4 eggs are laid and are cared for by both parents.

♂♀ **Pygmy Long-tailed Sunbird**
Anthreptes platura

Sunbirds are the ecological counterparts in the Old World to hummingbirds in the New. Like hummingbirds, their principal food is nectar, which is sucked from flowers with their tube-like tongues. Insects and some fruit are also eaten. 'Pygmy' refers to their size – males are 16–18cm (6.3–7in) with tail plumes of 9–10cm (3.5–3.9in), which the drab-coloured 8cm (3.1in) females lack. The males' long tail feathers are moulted outside the breeding season. This species is found in the arid woodlands of northern Uganda, north-west Kenya, Sudan, Ethiopia, Somalia and east to south-west Arabia. A long, pendant nest is

constructed from a branch by the female, which is fed by her mate as she cares for 2–3 eggs.

♂♀ **Rainbow Lory or Lorikeet**
Trichoglossus haematodus

All of the 54 species in the Lory family or Loriidae are characterized by their brush-tipped tongues, which help them to extract nectar and pollen from plants. They also feed on fruit, insects and their larvae in their native habitat of forests, gardens and parks. These aptly named arboreal parrots, which reach about 26cm (10.2in) when adult, are found in northern and eastern Australia, New Guinea and Indonesia. They are usually seen in pairs or in flocks of up to 100. These noisy, gregarious birds nest high above the ground in holes in trees where the female lays 2 eggs that she then incubates.

♂♀ **Raven** *Corvus corax*

The Raven can be found over most of the northern hemisphere and in many cultures has been unfairly associated with bad luck and witchcraft. In medieval Europe it was the traditional 'gallows-bird', often seen perching next to what it took to be carrion. It is resident throughout its range and frequents cliffs, mountainous areas and woodland slopes. It may also scavenge in villages. Pairs mate for life and in spring the female builds or renovates a nest built in a previous year and lays 3–7 eggs. The young are fed by both parents. Ravens are intelligent omnivores and reach 66cm (26in) in length.

♂♀ **Red-breasted Flycatcher** *Ficedula parva*

The Red-breasted Flycatcher is the smallest of the European flycatchers and measures just 11.5cm (about 4.5in). It usually ventures no farther west than southern Germany where it is known as the *Zwergschnapper*. It takes many small flying insects on the wing by sallying from its perch and returning to eat its catch. Flycatchers are found in deciduous forests where they nest in holes in trees, in nest boxes or in open nests they have built against tree trunks. Between 4–6 eggs are laid. The female lacks the orange/red breast of the male.

♂♀ **Red Kite** *Milvus milvus*

About 400–500 years ago Red Kites were almost as common in London as pigeons are today but now the small British population is confined to Wales. They are more widely distributed in continental Europe, North Africa and western Asia and are inhabitants of woodland and open country, preying on a wide variety of small animals and carrion. Northern populations form flocks of 50–200 and migrate to the south of this range in winter. Red Kites breed in April–May, often using abandoned nests. They produce 1–5 eggs, which are mainly incubated by the female. The young are fed by both parents. They eventually grow to 61–66cm (24–26in) – the female is larger than the male – with a wingspan of 145–155cm (57–61in).

♂♀ Red-tailed Tropicbird *Phaethon rubricauda*

The Red-tailed Tropicbird is one of 3 species of tropicbird and reaches 41cm (16in) in length to which can be added its distinctive red tail streamers of up to 35cm (13.8in). The plumes are present in both sexes and are highly prized as ornaments by the Polynesians. These normally solitary seabirds occur in the Indian and Pacific Oceans where they fish by hovering over the sea before plunge-diving to catch fish and crustaceans. Tropicbirds lay a single egg under a rocky overhang on bare ground. The chick is fed on regurgitated fish. The birds' shrill call, akin to the sound of a bosun's whistle, has earned them the name 'bosunbird'; sailors also call them 'marlin-spikes' due to the shape of their tails.

♂♀ Redwing *Turdus iliacus*

In flight the red wing linings and flanks of this thrush are conspicuous, and give it its name. Redwings breed in the woods and forests of northern Europe and Asia where they feed on worms, insects and berries. They migrate south and west in large flocks in October–November to overwinter, returning to their northern nesting ground in March–April. A nest is built in a tree and the female lays 2–8 eggs that are cared for by both parents. The length of the Redwing is 21cm (8.3in).

♂♀ Rhea *Rhea americana*

The flightless South American Rhea occupies a similar ecological niche in the New World to the African Ostrich in the Old. Rheas are powerful runners and range over the pampas and highland plateaus east of the Andes in flocks of 20–30. Like Ostriches, they are also omnivores and adults reach 1.5m (4.9ft) in height and weigh up to 25kg (over 55lb), making them the largest American bird. In the breeding season males display competitively and the victor gathers a 'harem' of several females that each lay their eggs on the ground into a nest previously selected by the male. A typical clutch is of about 12–30 eggs. These are then incubated by the male alone, who also cares for the young.

♂♀ Robin *Erithacus rubecula*

For reasons that remain obscure – possibly as a hangover from an earlier religion – this small member of the thrush family (Turdidae) has come to symbolize Christmas in many western countries. The 14cm (5.5in) Robin is widely distributed throughout Europe, the Mediterranean islands and across much of Asia as far as western Siberia. It inhabits forests, mixed woods and gardens. It is a ground feeder eating insects, spiders, worms, snails and berries and at times is extremely aggressive to others of its own species, presenting its distinctive red breast as a threat display to intruders. Solitary in winter, Robins form pairs in March–April and after mating the female builds a nest near the ground in a bank or hollow tree where she incubates 3–9 eggs. The chicks are subsequently fed by both parents. This

name is also used for the American Robin *Turdus migratorius*, a thrush.

♂♀ Rufous-tailed Jacamar *Galbula ruficauda*

Jacamars feed on flying insects such as bees, wasps, butterflies and dragonflies that they seize on with an audible snap of the bill, having often engaged in aerobatics in the chase. They return to their accustomed perch to consume their prey. This species breeds during March–July and pairs build a burrow 30–45cm (11.8-17.7in) long in a bank that opens out into a nesting chamber at the end where the female lays 2–4 eggs. This burrow is used in consecutive years. The eggs are incubated by both parents. Rufous-tailed Jacamars reach 23–28cm (9–11in) in length, including their long, tapering tail feathers and long, slender bills. They inhabit the tropical forests and woodlands of Central and South America and those of the islands of Trinidad and Tobago.

♂♀ Sand Martin or Bank Swallow *Riparia riparia*

The Sand Martin is a small member of the swallow family (Hirundinidae) that measures 12–14cm (4.7–5.5in) with a wingspan of 25–28cm (10–11in). It can be found over a wide range which includes the temperate regions of Eurasia and North America. It is a migratory species and European populations winter in Africa. Sand Martins return to their northern breeding grounds in April–May and excavate a burrow about 1m (3.3ft) long in a sand or mud bank with a nesting chamber at the end where the female lays 3–4 eggs. These are incubated in turn by both parents and the young are fed by both parents. Sand Martins breed in colonies and feed on the wing catching a variety of small insects.

♂♀ Scarlet Ibis *Eudocimus ruber*

In the breeding season, which coincides with the annual tropical rains, vividly coloured Scarlet Ibises form densely packed breeding colonies numbering many hundreds of birds. Each female lays 2–4 eggs that she incubates in turn with her mate. The young eventually reach their full size of 52–68cm (20.5–26.8in) with wingspans of 95cm (37.4in). They are distributed along coastal stretches of north-eastern South America and south-eastern Brazil where they feed in shallow water on amphibians, fish, molluscs, crustaceans and insects.

♂♀ Scarlet Macaw *Ara macao*

The Scarlet Macaw is one of the gaudiest and better known parrots and though its breeding range has been much reduced due to deforestation and also the taking of birds to supply the pet trade it can still be found in flocks of up to 20 birds in suitable habitats in Mexico, Central and South America south to Brazil. It is among the largest of parrots and an adult measures about 85cm (33.5in). It feeds on nuts, berries, fruit and seeds. Scarlet Macaws pair at the beginning of the breeding season and

after mating the female lays 2–4 eggs in a hollow tree or rock crevice. The female incubates the eggs while being fed by her mate. The young, which are born featherless and blind, are cared for by both parents.

♂♀ Secretary Bird *Sagittarius serpentarius*

In the popular imagination of bygone days secretaries were seen as rather stiff individuals in starched white shirts and black trousers with quill pens stuck behind their ears and it was this that gave rise to this bird's common name. It is a large terrestrial bird of prey and the only extant member of the family Sagittariidae. A powerful long-legged bird, about 1.2m (3.9ft) in length, it can, however, soar like a buzzard on its broad wings which span 2.1m (nearly 6.9ft). Secretary Birds live on the plains of Africa south of the Sahara and may walk several kilometres a day in search of any small ground-dwelling prey, taking snakes, lizards, mice, grasshoppers and birds' eggs. They have stout, heavily scaled legs to protect them from snakes which they kill by stamping on them or by flailing them against the ground and then swallowing them whole. In the breeding season a large nest of sticks and twigs is built in the top of a tree. Some 2–3 eggs are laid and cared for by both parents.

♂♀ Serin *Serinus serinus*

The Serin is a small European finch and the female is slightly duller in colour than the male. Both measure about 11.5cm (4.5in) and are to be found among the parks, gardens and vineyards of southern Europe during the winter months, extending this range to include most of continental Europe from late March onwards. At the start of the breeding season the female builds a small nest lined with feathers and hair in a tree. She lays 3–5 eggs that she mainly incubates alone while her mate feeds her. Serins return to their winter quarters in October.

♂♀ Shelduck *Tadorna tadorna*

A disused rabbit burrow is often the nesting site for the Shelduck. During May–June the female lays 7–16 eggs, which she cares for alone while the male (Sheldrake) stands guard nearby. Soon after hatching the ducklings follow their parents to the water and feed on various small molluscs, crustaceans, vegetable matter and insects. Shelducks are slightly smaller than geese and reach 61cm (24in) in length. The female is slightly smaller than the male. They range from the coasts of Europe east as far as Central China where they are also found inland on salt lakes. They migrate to warmer latitudes to pass the winter.

♂♀ Skylark *Alauda arvensis*

The breeding range of the Skylark extends from western Europe east to eastern China and Japan. Most migrate to the south of this range in the autumn for the winter months. The Skylark is

Have you been keeping track of the snails as you progress?
By now you should have found six including this one, which appears
to be having a whale of a time. You may need to thrash around
to name the pair of birds shown here and do keep an eye out
for a herald of spring, a pointed pet and an
idolatrous ichthyomorph.

renowned for its melodious song, which it gives during its songflight for minutes on end as it ascends, hovers and then descends over its breeding territory. The nest is well hidden in grass and the female lays 3–7 eggs. The young leave the nest after about 11 days and hide in the surrounding grass while their parents continue to feed them on various small insects and seeds. Both sexes are similar in plumage and are about 18cm (just over 7in) in length.

♂♀ Smew *Mergus albellus*

The Smew is a small duck that is adapted to diving and mainly lives on small fish and other invertebrates. It is found on lakes and rivers in northern Asia as far west as Russia, northern Finland and isolated parts of Sweden. The Smew is also seen on reservoirs, gravel pits and along coasts and estuaries during the winter months. It measures about 40cm (15.8in). The female nests in a tree hollow near water and lays 6–11 eggs. Smews are sexually dimorphic.

♂♀ Snow Bunting *Plectrophenax nivalis*

Snow Buntings breed in the colder parts of the northern hemisphere but migrate south for the winter. A nest made from moss, grass and lichen is lined with feathers and hairs and is well concealed under rocks or boulders. The female lays 4–6 eggs. Fifteen days after hatching the chicks leave the nest and join their parents feeding on insects and other small invertebrates. A Snow Bunting is 15.2cm (6in) in length; the sexes have different plumage.

♂♀ Snow Goose *Anser caerulescens*

Hunters know the Snow Goose by its Native American name of 'Wavey'. When it is in its blue-grey colour phase, it is commonly called the Blue Goose. It breeds colonially on open tundra and lake islands in the Canadian Arctic and extreme eastern Siberia and migrates each winter in large flocks to the coastal regions of the Gulf of Mexico and Japan. Some 4–6 eggs are laid in a ground-built nest and cared for by the female while the gander is often on guard nearby until the goslings hatch. The adult Snow Goose is 64–78cm (25.2–30.7in).

♂♀ Snowy Owl *Nyctea scandiaca*

The preferred diet of the Snowy Owl is the lemming, but in times of scarcity it readily preys on other mammals as large as the Arctic hare and also on the young of various birds such as gulls, geese and ptarmigan. It lives on the Arctic tundra and barren hills with low scrub. It winters further south in Europe, Asia and North America. Snowy Owls measure 54–66cm (about 21–26in) and have a wingspan of 135cm (over 53in). Pairs breed in May and a shallow nest scrape or depression on open ground is used. The female lays 4–10 eggs – more in years of plentiful food, that is, lemming years. These are incubated by the female

alone while she is fed by her mate. The first youngster to hatch grows more quickly than the last to hatch and the latter does not survive when food is in short supply.

♂♀ Spoonbill *Platalea leucorodia*

Spoonbills feed in shallow, open water, estuaries and marshes. They mostly have distinctive white plumage (pink in 1 species) and long, spatulate bills, which they use to feed on crustaceans and small fish by sweeping it from side to side. When they are excited they make a clattering noise with this bill. The sexes are similar and mature Spoonbills have a yellowish tinge at the base of the neck and a pendant crest. During the breeding season they form nesting colonies in reed beds. They are widely distributed from Central and southern Europe to Asia, and are also found in Africa. An adult typically measures about 87cm (34.3in).

♂♀ Standard-winged Nightjar *Macrodipteryx longipennis*

The Nightjar is also known as a 'goatsucker' and 'nighthawk' and is a nocturnal, insectivorous bird mainly active at dawn and dusk. Although it has a small bill it has an enormous gape surrounded by a few long, sensitive, rictal bristles that help to funnel prey into the mouth. The male Standard-winged Nightjar is remarkable for the greatly elongated shafts of his ninth primary feathers. They are developed early in the breeding season and used in sexual display. These ornamental plumes double his body length from 23cm (9in) to 46cm (18in). This African species breeds from Senegal to southern Ethiopia and northern Kenya, where it can be found in bush, grassland and savanna woodlands. These secretive birds are probably polygamous and after mating the female lays 1–2 eggs on the bare ground that she cares for alone.

♂♀ Storm Petrel *Hydrobates pelagicus*

Storm Petrels are pelagic and are distributed in the north-east Atlantic Ocean and the western Mediterranean Sea and at 14–18cm (5.5–7in) are the smallest European seabirds. They winter off the west and south coasts of Africa. They feed on plankton and fragments of fish, squid and crustaceans, which they pick from the surface of the sea. They only return to the land to breed in April–May on offshore rocky islands where they use discarded rabbit burrows or rock crevices to lay 1 or occasionally 2 eggs, which are incubated by both parents.

♂♀ Sulphur-crested Cockatoo *Cacatua galerita*

The Sulphur-crested Cockatoo is one of 18 species of the cockatoo family – Cacatuidae – and is one of the most easily recognized parrots and well known as a cage bird. In captivity it has been recorded as living for more than 50 years. It is found in

northern and eastern Australia, Tasmania, New Guinea and the Aru Islands, and has also been introduced into New Zealand. It lives in open forest, savanna, woodland and farmland and often forms large, noisy flocks numbering several hundred birds. It only pairs up during the breeding season. An adult is 50cm (19.7in) long and feeds on a variety of seeds, fruit, nuts, insects and other plant matter. Sulphur-crested Cockatoos nest in a hole in a tree where 2–3 eggs are laid.

♂♀ Toco Toucan *Ramphastos toco*

A common Toucan that inhabits tropical forest and plantations between northern Argentina and the Guianas. Its principal diet is fruit – especially capsicums – occasionally supplemented by insects, frogs, reptiles and small birds and their eggs. It is the largest species of Toucan, reaching 61–65cm (24–25.6in) in length and the bill is about 19cm (nearly 7.5in). The large, distinctive bill is remarkably light; the interior is formed of a honeycomb-like structure, which gives it great rigidity. The birds nest in holes in trees where the female lays 2 eggs that she subsequently incubates together with the male. The young are born with small bills, which gradually develop over 7 weeks.

♂♀ Wallcreeper *Tichodroma muraria*

Wallcreepers are renowned for their climbing abilities on steep rock faces or old buildings while searching for insects using their long, thin, de-curved bills. They are distributed from China west through Asia to Central and southern Europe and are about 16.5cm (6.5in) long. After a showy display flight when the male shows off his crimson and black wings a nest is built of grass and moss in a rock crevice. Some 3–5 eggs are laid and incubated by the female. When these hatch the young are fed by both parents for a further 23–25 days.

♂♀ Wandering Albatross *Diomedea exulans*

The Wandering Albatross is the largest member of its family (Diomedeidae), reaching 110–135cm (43.3–53.2in) and weighing 6.8–9kg (nearly 15–20lb) with a huge wingspan of 3.5m (11.5ft), which makes it the longest winged bird. It soars effortlessly over the southern oceans between 60°S–30°S latitude that are its home and feeding grounds. These latitudes include the Roaring Forties and the Howling Fifties – the strong winds that are essential for soaring. They feed principally on squid, taken by surface-seizing or by making shallow-plunges. Wandering Albatrosses only come to land when they are mature enough to breed (5–7 years old). They nest colonially on sub-Antarctic islands and mating involves complex courtship ceremonies with ritual bill clapping and wing-spreading displays. A single egg is laid on a truncated mud cone nest and incubated for extended periods by both parents. The chick is fed by its parents for approximately 8 months. Adults breed in alternate years.

♂♀ Whiskered or Lesser Tree Swift
Hemiprocne comata

Tree Swifts – also known as 'crested swifts', though their head crest is not evident in flight – are more brightly coloured than true swifts and are to be found in the forests of south-east Asia and New Guinea. They feed on a variety of flying insects, but unlike the true swifts, often spend some time preening and resting on dead tree limbs. These small, 15.3cm (6in) birds are found in clearings and forest edges in Sumatra, Borneo and the Philippines. In the breeding season a small, paper-thin, cup-shaped nest is stuck on the side of a thin branch and the single egg that just fits is glued in with saliva for safety and incubated by both the male and female.

♂♀ White-barred Piculet
Picumnus cirratus

The White-barred Piculet is a tiny woodpecker, 9cm (3.5in) in length. It is widely distributed in eastern South America from Guyana to northern Argentina. It frequents woodland and forests, diligently searching bamboo or the smaller twigs and branches of trees, even hanging upside down, and taking insects and their larvae. White-barred Piculets excavate nesting holes in bamboo stems.

♂♀ White-browed Wood-swallow
Artamus superciliosus

Wood-swallows are unrelated to true swallows but may be distant cousins to starlings (Sturnidae). The nomadic White-browed Wood-swallow is 19–21cm (7.5–8.3in) long and is widely distributed in eastern and inland Australia where it frequents open woodland and cultivated areas, sometimes forming mixed flocks with Masked Wood-swallows *A. personatus*. It is entirely insectivorous, but its brush-tipped tongue may help in taking nectar. Wood-swallows are the only songbirds to have powder-down feathers and they roost in small groups, sometimes tightly together, in a tree hollow or foliage. Breeding seems governed by the arrival of the rains when a scanty nest of twigs, grass stems and rootlets is constructed. Some 2–3 eggs are laid.

♂♀ White Pelican *Pelecanus onocrotalus*

The Pelican is often used in heraldry, particularly on the arms of ecclesiastics, to denote piety due to the legend that the females would pierce their breasts to feed their young on their own blood. This Old World species is a native of Asia and Africa but a small number also breed in the Danube delta and Greece. The Pelican has a large, distensible, membranous pouch beneath its bill that it uses as a scoop to collect fish. Pelicans often fish co-operatively in small groups, herding fish to shallow water where they are more easily dealt with. These birds are about 1.5m (5ft) in length and have large wingspans of about 2.7m (9ft). They are expert and powerful flyers, though they may appear clumsy and ungainly on land. The female lays 2–4 eggs in a nest crudely constructed from sticks where the young are later cared for by both parents.

♂♀ White Stork *Ciconia ciconia*

In March–April flocks of White Storks arrive in Central and eastern Europe and western Asia from their winter quarters in sub-equatorial Africa. They renovate earlier nests or build new ones, often on roofs or chimneys in towns and villages. A stork nest on your house is believed to bring good fortune, which is possibly another facet of the popular legend that storks are responsible for bringing babies. Some 4–7 eggs are laid and incubated by both parents. The young are fed on regurgitated food and fledge in 8–9 weeks. When fully grown White Storks measure 102cm (40.3in) long and stand 120cm (47.3in) high. They feed mainly while wading, taking various small aquatic animals, insects, frogs and reptiles. They are virtually voiceless and their only loud sound is made when they clatter their bills at the nest. In August–September they depart once more for their winter quarters.

♂♀ White-throated Bulbul *Criniger flaveolus*

Noisy flocks of White-throated Bulbuls often travel in groups of 6–15 birds and live in the tropical forests of northern India, Burma and Thailand where they forage for insects, berries and wild figs. They frequently form mixed flocks with other species. In the breeding season 3–4 eggs are laid in a well-concealed nest, about 1m (3.3ft) from the ground, built beforehand by both parents, who share the incubation. The young are fed by their parents on insects. White-throated Bulbuls are 23cm (9in) in length.

♂♀ Whooping Crane *Grus americana*

The Whooping Crane is so-called on account of its call, which carries for some distance. It is one of the rarest birds in the world and has been close to extinction in recent times. Once widespread from the Mackenzie River in Canada south to Illinois and Iowa in the USA by 1938 there were only 14 birds left in the wild. As a result of rigorous protection and a foster-breeding programme this figure had risen to 59 by 1971, to 70 by 1977 and 110 by 1987 with perhaps 2 dozen more in captivity. Happily, their numbers continue to increase. Their decline was partly due to changing ecological conditions, which were severely aggravated by hunting, and to land cultivation by settlers. As the adults are long-lived, pairs normally only produce 1–2 offspring each year. The Whooping Crane breeds in the North-west Territories of Canada and winters on the Gulf Coast of south-eastern Texas. It is the tallest North American bird standing 1.5m (4.9ft) with a wingspan of 2.1m (6.9ft).

♂♀ Wood Duck *Aix sponsa*

The breeding plumage of the male Wood Duck (drake) is perhaps the most handsome and striking of any member of the duck family. However, during the period of 'eclipse' from June–October drakes moult into a female-type plumage. Wood Ducks breed in the eastern and north western parts of the USA and southern Canada and in autumn migrate south reaching as far as southern California, Florida and parts of the Caribbean to winter. After mating the female (duck) lays 8–14 eggs in a lofty nest in a tree hole or often in an abandoned woodpecker hole. The eggs are incubated by the female. After hatching, with the encouragement of the female, the ducklings leap from the nest. The impact of their fall is softened by their down and they quickly follow their mother to water where they soon learn to find their own food. When fully grown they measure 50cm (19.7in) in length. They feed on plant matter supplemented with insects, molluscs and worms in the summer months.

♂♀ Woodpigeon *Columba palumbus*

Woodpigeons originally made their home in the mixed woodlands of Europe and their range also extended east to Central Russia and northern India and south to the Mediterranean and North Africa. Changes in land management and agricultural practices in recent years have greatly helped in the increase of their numbers and in some areas they have become a serious agricultural pest feeding on cereal crops. Northern populations overwinter in the south or south-west of their range and arrive back in their breeding areas in early spring. A flimsy stick nest is constructed by the female with material brought by the male and (usually) 2 eggs are incubated in turn by both parents. The young (squabs) are fed at first on a substance produced by the adult known as 'pigeon's milk'– a whitish fluid produced in the crop lining of both sexes containing cheese-like particles. A second, and occasionally a third, brood is produced from late summer. Woodpigeons grow to 40.5cm (16in) and have wingspans of 46cm (18.1in).

♂♀ Wren or Winter Wren
Troglodytes troglodytes

The range of this small 9.5–11.5cm (3.7–4.5in) bird, which weighs only 8–9 g (0.3oz), includes most of Eurasia as far east as Japan. It also occurs in Iceland and is widespread in southern Canada, eastern USA and the Pacific coast. It forages in undergrowth for spiders, insects and their larvae, seeds and berries. It has a loud musical song for its size and is also recognizable by its cocked tail. It is believed that the male is polygamous and in April may build several dome-shaped nests for other females to lay their clutch of 4–16 eggs. The eggs are incubated by the female alone and the parents feed the young until they leave the nest at 16–17 days.

♂♀ Wrybill *Anarhynchus frontalis*

The Wrybill is unique in the avian world in having a bill curved 20° to the right, a feature evident even in newly hatched chicks. It uses its bill in a scythe-like fashion for probing under stones in shallow water to find the aquatic insects on which it feeds.

Birdbrains might recall meeting at least one of these creatures
before in this book. There's also a lupine lookout,
three long-legged leapers, a malodorous American and a
puffed-up porcine plaything. This snail seems to have made
a tasty morsel for someone.

Also known as the Wrybill Plover this bird is found only in New Zealand where it winters on the coasts of North Island and returns to its breeding grounds on South Island in October. The female lays 2–3 camouflaged eggs on the shingle of a large estuary. Wrybills are 20cm (7.9in) long.

♂♀ Yellow-backed Sunbird or Crimson Sunbird
Aethopyga siparaja

The brilliantly coloured male Yellow-backed Sunbird is much more conspicuous than the drab female and, at 13.3cm (5.2in) including his elongated tail feathers, is longer than his 10.8cm (4.3in) mate. These birds are to be found in the forests and cultivated lands of India, south-eastern Asia, Borneo, Java, Sumatra, Sulawesi and the Philippines at altitudes of up to 1200m (3937ft). Their principal diet is nectar, which is sucked up with their tubular tongues, but if the nectar cannot be reached they puncture the base of the flower to get at it. They travel around their territory each day in search of suitable flowers. In the breeding season a pendant, pear-shaped nest suspended from a branch is built by the female. She lays 2–3 eggs that she incubates and rears alone while being fed by her mate.

♂♀ Yellow-billed Oxpecker or Tickbird
Buphagus africanus

The African Yellow-billed Oxpecker specializes in feeding on lice and ticks, which it finds by clambering on large mammals such as buffalo, zebra and giraffe. These large savanna-dwelling animals tolerate this – even intrusions into nostrils and ears – as the birds rid them of bothersome parasites and alert them to approaching danger with their alarm calls, though they also open sores by pecking at flesh. Yellow-billed Oxpeckers are members of the starling family (Sturnidae) and nest in hollow trees, rock cavities or under the eaves of houses where the female lays 2–5 eggs, which she incubates. Fully grown birds measure 23cm (9in).

MAMMALS

The 4008 known species of the class Mammalia are divided into about 120 families and 20 orders and are distinguished from the rest of the animal world by the fact that they suckle their young with milk-secreting glands (mammae) from which they derive their name. Mammals evolved from reptilian ancestors between the early Jurassic period (around 180 million years ago) and the late Cretaceous period (around 70 million years ago). They are enormously varied in size from the tiny Kitti's Hog-nosed or Bumblebee Bat *Craseonycteris thonglongyai*, which is only the size of a large Bumblebee with a body just 33mm (1.3in) long

and a weight of less than 2g (0.07oz), to the largest creature ever to exist – the giant Blue Whale *Balaenoptera musculus*, which reaches lengths of about 25m (82ft) and a weight of up to 150 tonnes (330,750lb). Mammals are diverse in form having evolved the ability to live on and beneath the land, in the sea and in the air. Humans *Homo sapiens* belong to this class and are believed to be the most intelligent creatures on the planet.

♂♀ Aardvark *Orycteropus afer*

The nocturnal Aardvark is found all over sub-Saharan Africa – anywhere, in fact, where it can find its preferred diet of termites, which it catches by breaking down termitaria with its powerful foreclaws and sweeping up the occupants with its 30cm (11.8in) long sticky tongue. Aardvarks spend their days in deep burrows with many 1m (3.3ft) long entrance tunnels and their nights in search of food. Normally solitary, they breed in May–November depending on the latitude. A single naked, flesh-coloured young is born. These creatures grow to 1–1.6m (3.3–5.2ft), with tails of 44.5–65cm (17.5–25.6in). Fossil remains of relatives of the Aardvark have been found in southern France, the Aegean Islands and eastern Europe. The common name, beloved of crossword puzzle compilers, is Afrikaans for 'earth-pig'.

♂♀ Aardwolf *Proteles cristatus*

Like the previous species, the principal diet of the nocturnal Aardwolf or 'earth-wolf' is termites, which it is able to detect with its acute hearing. It also eats other insects as well and laps them off the ground with its tongue, which is covered with sticky saliva. It seeks insects in a territory surrounding its den, which is often a disused aardvark burrow. This area is marked with a pungent scent from its anal gland that is also used as a defence against its main predators such as lions, leopards, spotted hyaenas and pythons. The Aardwolf lives on the savannas and arid plains of sub-Saharan Africa and grows to a length of 55–80cm (21.7–31.5in) with a tail of 20–30cm (7.9–11.8in). Little breeding information is available about this shy and elusive animal, but it seems that 2–4 young are produced and fed on regurgitated food by their parents.

♂♀ Addax *Addax nasomaculatus*

In common with many desert dwellers, the nomadic Addax can go without drinking as it derives all the moisture it needs from the plants it eats. This antelope has large hooves suitable for walking on the sands of the southern Sahara Desert where it is found in small numbers. Its large horns of 60–109cm (23.6–42.9in) are present in both sexes. It spends most of the day sheltering from the fierce desert heat and is active in the evening and early morning. A single young is produced. The Addax grows to about 1.3m (4.3ft) with a tail length of 25–35cm (9.9–13.8in). There are probably fewer than 1000 of these antelopes left in the wild and the extinction of this species seems imminent, though they are being bred successfully in captivity with a view to reintroduction.

♂♀ African Buffalo *Synceros caffer*

Unlike the Indian Buffalo *Bubalus arnee*, the African Buffalo has never been domesticated and is to be found in herds sparsely scattered over most of sub-Saharan Africa, apart from South Africa. Both males (bulls) and females (cows) have horns, which are as large as 1.6m (5.3ft) in mature males. Males can measure 3m (9.8ft). A single calf can be born at any time of the year. The herd is always to be found close to water where it drinks regularly and wallows in the mud. The African Buffalo is a powerful beast and all but the sick and young are safe from attack even by lions.

♂♀ African Elephant *Loxodonta africana*

This is the world's largest land animal. A mature male stands up to 4m (13.1ft) tall at the shoulder and weighs as much as 6.5 tonnes (14,333lb). Both sexes possess tusks that in the male can grow to 3.4m (11.2ft) and which, despite strict controls, are still the prize of poachers who are solely responsible for the rapid decline of this species. These vegetarian animals have appropriately huge appetites and consume daily as much as 200kg (441lb) of fruit, leaves, roots, shoots, bark and twigs, which are grasped with their extraordinarily dexterous trunks. They are capable of breaking down trees with trunks of 1m (3.3ft) diameter and tend to destroy as much as they consume, frequently damaging crops. African Elephants live in family troops of 10–50 animals led by a mature female (cow). Mature males (bulls or tuskers) form separate troops and old males are solitary. African Elephants breed every 4–6 years, mating in all seasons. A single young (calf), which weighs up to 120kg (264.6lb), is born and remains with its mother for over 2 years. The animals bathe every day if they can and frequently cover themselves in dust or mud as a protection against the sun and insects in the bush, savanna and forest of sub-Saharan Africa where they live. African Elephants have much larger ears than Asian elephants *Elephas maximas* and these are sometimes used as giant fans to cool themselves. Generally, they have not been domesticated, unlike Asian elephants, but this is probably due more to cultural reasons than to any inherent untameability.

♂♀ African Wild Ass *Equus africanus*

The African Wild Ass is the ancestor of the smaller domestic donkey and stands about 1.2m (3.9ft) high at the shoulder. It is now very rare throughout its range which, for the most part, comprises desert regions at elevations of about 2000m (6562ft) where fresh water and vegetation are scarce. It is an agile creature well adapted to rugged terrain and is most active at night and in the comparative cool of dawn and dusk. Today probably no more than 3000 remain, distributed mostly over Sudan, Somalia and Ethiopia, but accurate figures as to its current status are impossible to come by. Some experts believe that many of the remaining herds consist of cross-breeds with domestic donkeys and despite being a protected species they are still prey to poachers, who kill them for their meat and hides. African Wild Asses live in herds of roughly 10–15 and a single young is produced.

♂♀ Agouti *Dasyprocta aguti*

The Agouti is a terrestrial rodent that is found in the forests and savannas of eastern Brazil, Venezuela and on the islands of the Lesser Antilles. It grows to 41–62cm (16 2–24.4in) and has a vestigial tail of 1–5cm (0.4–1.2in). It feeds on fruit, leaves and roots, sometimes causing damage to banana and sugar cane crops. Agoutis breed twice a year and 2–4 young are born in a burrow among boulders, roots or in a riverbank. They are shy animals that can run swiftly and leap up to 2m (6.6ft). Although their status is poorly documented, they are believed to be declining in numbers due to the loss of their habitat and to serious depredations from hunting.

♂♀ American Beaver *Castor canadensis*

Much of the North American interior was first opened up by trappers hunting the valuable pelts of this rodent, which formerly ranged from northern Canada to Mexico. American Beavers have also been exploited for their musky glandular secretion known as 'castoreum' with which they mark out their territory and which has been used in perfume making. 'Beaver' has become a byword for industriousness and they are well known for building extensive dams from logs and mud to create small lakes that constitute their ideal environment and that do not completely freeze in winter. In these lakes they construct domed habitations or 'lodges' up to 2m (6.7ft) high of sticks and plastered mud with several underwater entrances and a dry interior nesting chamber. Beavers mate in midwinter and (usually) 4 young (kits) are born that grow to an adult size of 60–103cm (23.6–31.5in), excluding their flat tails of 25–45cm (9.9–17.7in). Beavers feed on the bark, twigs and roots of trees, particularly willow and aspen, which they store beneath their lakes. They are capable of gnawing through trunks of 70cm (27.6in) with their razor-sharp teeth. In alarm they slap the water explosively with their tails, which can be heard for 800m (almost 0.5 mile). They can swim for a similar distance underwater, staying submerged for 15 minutes.

♂♀ American Manatee or Wide-nosed Manatee *Trichecus manatus*

This largely nocturnal creature, which was once hunted for its flesh, hide and oil, is today under threat from pollution, becoming ensnared in fishing nets and drowning and from being lacerated by the propellers of powerboats. American Manatees, which have 3–4m (9.8-13.1ft) long bodies and oval tail flukes, are found either singly or in groups of up to 20 in the coastal waters from Florida south to Guyana where they feed on aquatic vegetation and consume 35–40kg (77.1–88.2lb) daily.

They swim slowly at about 8km/h (nearly 5mph) and rise regularly to the surface to breathe. In the breeding season males (bulls) engage in fights to mate with females (cows). A single young (calf) is born and is helped to the surface by its mother to take its first breath; it remains with her for 2 years.

♂♀ American Mink *Mustela vison*

The mink coat was formerly a symbol of wealth and since the American Civil War (1861–65) these animals have been bred in captivity to supply the demands of the furrier. The sumptuous sheen that makes their pelt so valuable is acquired in late autumn. In February–March the normally solitary male seeks a mate. A litter of up to 10 blind kits is produced. When adult they measure 30–50cm (11.8–19.7in) with 13–23cm (5.1–9in) tails, though the females are smaller. American Mink are excellent swimmers and ruthless and wasteful killers, preying on a wide variety of small mammals, fish, crustaceans, birds, snakes and frogs. American Mink are found throughout North America with the exception of the arid south-west.

♂♀ Arctic Fox or White Fox or Polar Fox *Alopex lagopus*

The coat of the Arctic Fox is grey-brown in summer, but becomes pure white in winter except in about 5 per cent of the population that have a smoky-grey coat throughout the year and are termed 'blue foxes'. Both types are hunted for their valuable pelts. Their distribution is circumpolar and they are opportunistic feeders, taking birds and their eggs, lemmings, voles and carrion and they often follow polar bears to feed on their leftovers. Smaller than red foxes, they measure 50–60cm (19.7–23.6in) with tails of 30cm (11.8in). A single litter of 4–14 pups is produced in April–June. They live in burrows and do not need to hibernate as they can tolerate temperatures as low as –50°C (–58°F).

♂♀ Asiatic Black Bear *Selenarctos thibetanus*

The Asiatic Black Bear is also known as the Moon Bear – no doubt due to the white crescent marking on its chest. The home of this creature is the forests and brushlands of Central and eastern Asia where during the summer it can be found at elevations as high as 3600m (over 11,800ft). It descends to 1500m (over 4900ft) to pass the winter months. Populations in warmer latitudes do not hibernate, but remain fairly active throughout the winter. Adults can measure up to 1.8m (5.9ft) and weigh 175kg (nearly 381.5lb) and, despite their name, their pelts can vary considerably from black through brown to a reddish colour. Their principal food is plant matter as well as birds' eggs and nestlings and they frequently raid crops in inhabited areas. They sometimes supplement this diet by killing livestock. The mating period is in June and July; the female gives birth to 1–2 cubs. The flesh and bones of this bear are an important ingredient in traditional Chinese medicine.

♂♀ Asiatic Elephant *Elephas maximas*

With the exception of the African Elephant *Loxodonta africana*, the Asiatic Elephant is the largest of all the terrestrial mammals with a maximum height of 3.1m (over 10ft) and a weight of up to 5 tonnes (11,025lb). The Asiatic Elephant is distinguished from the African by its smaller size, considerably smaller ears, a trunk with only one finger-like protrusion at its tip and only rudimentary tusks in the female. In the wild it usually lives in a forest habitat in small herds of related individuals – predominantly females (cows) and their young (calves) – led by an elderly female. The males (bulls) tend to live apart from the herd, approaching the females mainly when they are in oestrus. Its principal diet is grass, leaves and fruit, though it often raids crops. Asiatic Elephants range from India, Sri Lanka and large parts of South-east Asia to Sumatra where they are endangered. They have been widely domesticated in these areas where their great strength is an enormous asset in land cultivation, forestry and as a means of transport. The important Hindu god Ganesa is represented as a four-armed man with the head of an elephant. He is worshipped as the god of wisdom, good luck and the remover of obstacles.

♂♀ Bactrian Camel or Two-humped Camel *Camelus bactrianus*

There are probably less than 500 wild Bactrian Camels in the Gobi Desert and even these are thought by some to be a feral population. Since at least the fourth century BC they have been used as beasts of burden capable of carrying 250kg (551.5lb) and have been exploited for their milk, meat, wool and hides. They are ideally adapted to harsh, arid environments and have broad feet suitable for walking on sand or snow, thick eyelashes and closable nostrils for keeping out windblown sand. They can go for prolonged periods without food or drink (*see* Dromedary). They range over Central Asia, China and Mongolia where they feed on almost any type of vegetation, which provides much of their moisture needs. The common ancestors of all the Camelids, including llama and alpaca, originated in North America where fossil remains have been found. Bactrian Camels measure 2.3–3.5m (7.5–11.3ft). A single young is produced.

♂♀ Barbary Ape *Macaca sylvanus*

'Barbary' was the name applied by the Europeans to the coastal states of North Africa, which were the original home of this tailless monkey that is not a true ape at all. It is also resident on the Rock of Gibraltar where it was probably introduced by the Moors in the first millennium AD, making it the only wild monkey species in Europe. Local legend has it that when the apes leave, the Rock's long association with the British will cease. Barbary Apes measure 55–75cm (21.7–29.5in). The small, tame Gibraltarian population aside, troops of 10–30 individuals roam within defined areas on the rocky hillsides of Morocco and northern Algeria feeding on plants and insects but their

Large, much-travelled seabird seeks mate – ancient mariner preferred.
Other birds must wait their turn. See if you can find a myopic crocodilian,
a volatile pisciform, a wee woodpecker and a healthy sacrifice.
Wild horses would not drag the answer to this riddle from me,
but the snail might be bought on tick.

numbers are declining due to loss of habitat and persecution by farmers whose crops they plunder. They mate throughout the year and a single young is born.

♂♀ Beech Marten *Martes foina*

The Beech Marten is a nocturnal, weasel-like carnivore that attains an adult size of 40–48cm (15.8-18.9in) with a tail of 22–26cm (8.7–10.2in). It is found on rocky hillsides up to elevations of 2400m (over 7874ft) and in deciduous woodland; it is distributed from the Himalaya and Altai Mountains west to Central and southern Europe as far as Spain and Portugal. It feeds on mice, shrews and birds, often eating berries to supplement this diet in autumn. It is not above raiding henhouses or plundering ducks' eggs. Beech Martens can frequently be found near human dwellings and make their dens in buildings and ruins. In the breeding season the female chooses a sheltered place to build a nest of leaves and grass where she gives birth to 3–7 blind young.

♂♀ Bighorn Sheep *Ovis canadensis*

The horns of a mature Bighorn male (ram) might measure more than 1m (3.3ft) along the outside curve of their spiral and give this species its name. The size of these horns establishes precedence within the flock but those of the female (ewe) are small and slender. Once abundant, today Bighorn Sheep probably number fewer than 40,000 and are restricted to the inaccessible areas of western North America from British Columbia possibly to Baja, California, where they wander in flocks of up to 15 often on seemingly sheer rock faces. Their decline seems due to overhunting and competition from domesticated livestock, but the species is now protected. They feed on grass, roots, berries and the buds of aspen and spruce (and sometimes cacti). The annual mating or 'rut' takes place in November–December when the rams become very aggressive and engage in extended, violent butting contests. But the victor does not seem to win a 'harem' of ewes, which are promiscuous and mate with several rams in turn. Some 1–2 lambs are born and rams eventually grow to about 1.6m (5.2ft) in length. The ewes are smaller.

♂♀ Bison *Bison bison*

Before the arrival of Europeans in North America there were perhaps more than 50 million Bison distributed over practically the whole continent. But by 1889 their numbers had been reduced to just 540 animals by hunting and by deliberate policies of extermination in order to subdue the Native American population. Today they are strictly protected and number about 50,000 in managed herds on the central prairie where they graze mainly on grass. They are the largest American land animal and a mature male measures up to 3.5m (11.5ft) in length. Bison live in nomadic herds and both sexes have short horns. In May a single calf is born.

♂♀ Black-backed Jackal *Canis mesomelas*

There are 2 populations of Black-backed Jackals, one of which is distributed in eastern Africa and the other in southern Africa. They inhabit the savannas, bush and open woodlands at altitudes of up to 2000m (6562ft). Black-backed Jackals are largely nocturnal, hunting either alone, in pairs or small packs, for animals of all kinds and especially for carrion. They are 70–100cm (27.6–39.4in) long with tails of 30–35cm (11.8-13.8in). Males and females pair for life and from June–October an average-sized litter of 5–7 is produced, which is fed at first on regurgitated food brought by the male. Black-backed Jackals' reputation for cowardice seems unfounded and they defend themselves by secreting a foul-smelling odour from a gland at the base of the tail against their enemies, which include leopards, cheetahs, eagles and pythons.

♂♀ Blackbuck *Antilope cervicapra*

Only the dominant male in each herd deserves the epithet black. The hornless females of this species of Asian antelope are a dull yellowish colour, as are the subordinate males, which have smaller horns than those of the head of the herd. His might measure 70cm (27.5in) long. The dark coloration and large horns only appear when a male takes charge of the herd of 15–50 on the death of the previous leader. All Blackbucks have the same distinctive pale underparts. They live on the grassy plains of India and Pakistan and, though once abundant, they are becoming increasingly rare today. In fact, the population of Blackbuck introduced into Texas in 1932 is now likely to outnumber that in its original homeland. Even though they were previously the prey of many of the large Indian carnivores the blame for their recent decline must be laid at the door of hunters and especially the increasing use of land for agriculture. Adult Blackbucks measure about 1.2m (nearly 4ft).

♂♀ Black Rhinoceros or Hook-lipped Rhinoceros *Diceros bicornis*

The total world population of the Black Rhinoceros is no more than 2000, though it was once the most numerous species of rhinoceros distributed in the thick bush and savanna of Africa from Sudan and southern Chad to South Africa. It browses on grass, twigs and other plants that it grasps with its prehensile, hook-shaped upper lip. It is solitary and will charge suspicious objects at speeds of up to 50km/h (31mph). It has acute hearing and smell but poor eyesight and is not black but rather grey-tinted from the mud that it habitually wallows in to rid itself of parasites. Black Rhinoceroses have 2, occasionally 3, horns, which rather than true horn are composed of keratin – a fibrous protein found in hair. Their numbers have declined alarmingly due to the predations of poachers who, despite strict controls, find illicit markets for the horns in the Middle East and in the Orient where powdered horn is still used in traditional medicines. Black Rhinoceroses mark their territory with dung heaps and sprayed urine. A single young is born, which when

adult eventually weighs as much as 1.6 tonnes (3528lb) and measures 360cm (141.8in) in length.

♂♀ Blue Monkey or Diademed Guenon *Cercopithecus mitis*

Despite its common name, the Blue Monkey is not really blue in colour. The alternative common name of Diademed Guenon refers to the supposed crown formed by its long forward-projecting forehead and eyebrow hair. Earlier this century these handsome monkeys were extensively hunted for the fur trade. Consequently, their numbers are diminished and their distribution fragmented to parts of Angola, Congo, Sudan, Ethiopia, Kenya, Uganda and Zambia. In the morning and late afternoon troops of up to 12 feed on shoots, bark, fruit, birds' eggs and insects in the upper tier of their forest habitat, but descend to the lower branches during the heat of the day. Blue Monkeys have an unrestricted breeding season; a single young is born that clings to its mother for the first month of its life. The size of the adult monkey varies among the various subspecies from 48–67cm (18.9–26.4in) in the males to 44–52cm (17.3–20.5in) in the females. Apart from humans, their principal enemies are leopards, eagles and pythons.

♂♀ Blue Wildebeest or Brindled Gnu *Connochaetes taurinus*

Blue Wildebeest live in enormous herds of up to 400,000 and, though at one time more abundant than today, populations in certain protected areas exceed 1.3 million individuals. They undertake long seasonal migrations of up to 1600km (about 993 miles) in search of their exclusive diet of grasses and they are distributed on the savannas of sub-equatorial eastern and southern Africa. The horns are present in both sexes but the females are smaller than the males, which grow to 2.4m (7.9ft) with tails of 1m (3.3ft). A single calf is born in November–January that becomes active within minutes of birth, but is especially vulnerable to lions, cheetahs, hyaenas and hunting dogs while young.

♂♀ Brown Bear *Ursus arctos*

The species *U. arctos* includes many subspecies, such as the Alaskan Brown Bear, the Grizzly Bear and the largest land carnivore, the Kodiak Bear, which measures up to 3m (9.8ft) and for which the greatest recorded weight is 750kg (1655lb). Bears of the tiny western European population are smaller in stature and now only exist in isolated montane areas. Although large, Brown Bears are capable of running at speeds of 48km/h (29.8mph). They have been consistently persecuted by man for centuries as they readily kill livestock, but they eat fruit, berries, nuts, fish, small animals and carrion as well. They are also inordinately fond of honey. As winter approaches they eat vast quantities that they store as fat to sustain them during a prolonged period of torpor rather than true hibernation. Brown Bears are very slow breeders and 1–4 (usually 2) cubs, weighing only 350g (12.3oz), are produced every 2–3 years. It was once believed that the tiny bear cubs were born formless and that their mother shaped them with her tongue, which is where we get the modern English expression 'lick into shape'. Brown Bears were used in the Middle Ages for the barbaric sport that later became known as 'bear-baiting' in which the hapless creatures – often whipped and blinded – were chained to a post and set upon by savage dogs, which fought to the death.

♂♀ Brown Hare
Lepus capensis (Lepus europaeus)

Hares are sometimes confused with rabbits but are easily distinguished by their greater size, longer ears and legs and by the fact that they do not live in colonies. Females usually give birth up to 3–4 times a year to 2–7 young (leverets) in an open nest (form) concealed in long grass. They are born open-eyed and fully furred, and are capable of moving about unaided almost from the moment of birth. A fully grown Brown Hare, which can be as long as 76cm (almost 30in), is capable of running at speeds of up to 65km/h (40mph) and can even swim to escape predators. Although a native of Eurasia, these largely nocturnal creatures have been introduced to most of the rest of the temperate regions of the world where they flourish in their habitat of open grassland, farmland and lightly wooded areas. In a legend of the Algonquins of North America, the hare Michabo pursued his pack of hunting wolves into a lake where they had chased their quarry, causing it to overflow and flood the world.

♂♀ Bushbuck Tragelaphus scriptus

The Bushbuck is a solitary, noctural antelope that is distributed in sub-Saharan Africa from Ethiopa to South Africa. Only the male has horns. These shy, elusive animals live in the undergrowth, forest margins and thickets up to elevations of 4000m (13,124ft) and they feed on a wide variety of plant matter. They are strong swimmers and are capable of jumping 2m (6.6ft) high fences, such as when fleeing from their principal enemy, the leopard. In the dry season the female gives birth to a single young. The larger males grow to 115–150cm (45.3–59in) in length.

♂♀ Cacomistle or Cacomixl or Ringtail
Bassariscus astutus

The anglicized 'Cacomistle' is derived from the Mexican name Cacomixl meaning rush-cat. It is a solitary and nocturnal carnivore that eats birds, eggs, lizards, frogs, small rodents and insects but also feeds on nuts, fruit and cereals when it finds them. The arboreal and secretive Cacomistle has a long, banded tail that accounts for half of its maximum total body length of up to 1m (3.3ft). It is distributed from Oregon, USA to southern Mexico and mates in February–March. Some 2–4 young are born. Cacomistles are hunted for their fur, which is popularly known as 'California Mink'.

♂♀ Capybara Hydrochaerus hydrochaeris

The order Rodentia comprises 50 per cent of all mammals. Rodents range in size from tiny mice to the semi-aquatic Capybara – the largest living rodent – which grows to 1–1.3m (3.3–5.5ft) long. Capybaras live in small groups or herds in wet areas with dense vegetation cover, swamps, rivers, marshes and grasslands with water from eastern Panama to northern Argentina. Their numbers have been declining in some parts in recent years due to hunting and to the draining of this land to make suitable pasture for cattle. Their natural enemy is the jaguar. Capybaras feed on a wide variety of plant matter, including grass and aquatic vegetation and they are excellent swimmers as their toes are partially webbed. In the mating season the male exudes a scent attractive to females from a gland on his nose. The female gives birth to 2–8 well-developed young in thick vegetation.

♂♀ Chamois Rupicapra rupicapra

Today the goat-like Chamois is only found in isolated populations in the high, inhospitable mountains of Europe and east to the Caucasus Mountains at, or above, the tree line, descending to as low as 800m (about 2624ft) in winter. The undersides of their hooves are soft and resilient enabling them to grip on smooth rocks and move about with astonishing agility. The horns are present in both sexes. Old males are solitary but the females and young live in herds of 15–30 and feed on flowers, herbs, shoots, moss and lichen. During the autumn rut males battle violently with each other for supremacy and in April–June (usually) a single young is produced that eventually grows to 90–130cm (35.5–51.2in). For centuries the Chamois has been extensively hunted for meat and tufts of its hair are the traditional cockades worn in alpine hats. Its cured skin is prized as shammy leather. Chamois have recently been introduced into New Zealand where they are thriving.

♂♀ Cheetah Acinonyx jubatus

The diurnal Cheetah is well known as the fastest land animal. It stalks its prey, which includes antelopes, hares, jackals and birds up to the size of young ostriches, to within 100m (about 328ft) and then takes them with a final sprint of up to 500m (over 1640ft) when it is capable of achieving speeds of over 100km/h (62mph). The prey is despatched by an efficient bite to the throat and is consumed on the spot. Once Cheetahs ranged all over Africa and large parts of south-western Asia and India but today they are restricted mostly to eastern and southern Africa where they are relatively abundant on reserves. The Arabian population became extinct in about 1950 and the tiny surviving Asiatic race is critically endangered. Cheetahs are animals of the desert and open savanna where they hunt by sight. For more than 4000 years they have been kept by man as hunting animals and the great Mogul Emperor Akbar (1542–1605) famously kept 1000 of them to hunt gazelles. Very few Cheetahs have been bred in captivity but in the wild mating seems to take place throughout the year and normally 2–4 young are born. The body of a fully grown male cheetah measures 110–140cm (43.3–55.2in) and its tail another 65–80cm (25.6–31.5in).

♂♀ Chimpanzee Pan troglodytes

The Chimpanzee is our closest relative. In the wild it lives in bands of 30–80 composed of several family groups in the tropical rainforests and wooded savannas of western and Central Africa at altitudes of up to 3300m (about 10,827ft). Its diet is mainly vegetarian, but it also takes birds' eggs and nestlings, insects – which are sometimes extracted from crevices with tools made from twigs – and occasionally it kills and eats young antelopes or baboons. Chimpanzees attract the anger of fruit farmers as they frequently raid crops – a habit that has contributed, with the progressive loss of their habitat, to their decline. They are active during the day on the ground and climbing and swinging in the trees. Each evening they construct a nest woven from leaves and branches in a tree to pass the night. Chimpanzees are promiscuous with several males mating with a receptive female in turn. A single young is born at any time of the year. It grows to a maximum height of 1.7m (nearly 5.5ft) when standing erect.

♂♀ Chinchilla Chinchilla laniger

The voluptuous, soft fur of the Chinchilla is the reason for its decline as it has been hunted since pre-Columbian times. The Incas allowed only royalty and the priesthood to wear garments made from its skin and today it is still one of the most highly prized furs. It is consequently bred in captivity to supply the demand of the trade. Up to 100 pelts from this animal, which only grows to 30–53cm (11.8-20.9in), including its tail, are needed to make a single coat. Once abundant in colonies of thousands, nowadays it only exists in the wild in isolated populations in the barren, inaccessible mountainous regions of the Andes in Bolivia and Chile at altitudes of up to 5000m (16,405ft). Accurate details of current numbers are hard to establish due to its remoteness. This crepuscular and nocturnal rodent lives in burrows or under rocks and feeds on any available vegetation. It usually gives birth to 2 young in April–May.

♂♀ Coati or Coatimundi Nasua nasua

As confirmed by its Latin name, the inquisitive Coati is nosy in both senses of the word. It uses its long, sensitive snout to forage about in leaf litter for all kinds of invertebrates, including venomous spiders. It also eats lizards, birds' eggs, land crabs, mice and fruit and it is active both in the trees and on the ground. Diurnal Coatis are found in the tropical forests of Central and South America and they seem to be extending their range north into Mexico and the southern United States. The aggressive males are solitary and larger than the females which,

There are at least five complete pairs of animals in this detail – but
that's strictly for the birds. You might continue your search with a trip
to the theatre where you could encounter the fiery couple who live
in the first house and their earthy neighbour at number ten.
Maybe you will find Columbine's sinuous spouse, a royal scavenger,
an insect with a jaundiced view on life, a chortling canine,
Athena's avian attribute . . . and a snail.

with their young, form troops of up to 40 individuals. The males briefly join the troop in the mating season. After copulation the female goes off alone and builds a nest in a tree where she gives birth to a litter of 2–7 of blind, naked young. Coatis measure 43–67cm (16.9–26.4in) and their long, banded tails are as long again.

♂♀ **Colocolo** *Dromiciops australis*

The Colocolo is found only in the lowlands and high-altitude forests of western Argentina and Chile. It is a marsupial and appears to be closely related to the opossum. It feeds on small invertebrates and plant matter, especially bamboo shoots. The breeding season for this adaptable animal is in spring and, though little information is available, it seems that as many as 5 young are produced that must cling to their mother's fur as, unlike most marsupials, Colocolos do not possess a true pouch. Adults vary in size from 11–12.5cm (4.3–4.9in) and have tails of 9–10cm (3.5–3.9in).

♂♀ **Common Dolphin** *Delphinus delphis*

Schools of Common Dolphins are frequently to be seen swimming alongside or riding the bow waves of oceangoing ships. They are pelagic and occur in all warm and temperate seas – most frequently in the Mediterranean and Black Seas – where they are extensively hunted. They are up to 2.5m (8.2ft) long and commonly live in groups of between 20–100, but sometimes form much larger schools. They feed on fish and squid and have been known to dive as deep as 280m (920ft) in search of them, staying submerged for 5 minutes at a time. Like other marine mammals, they must surface periodically to breathe. Common Dolphins find their prey by echolocation. They produce a series of clicks and whistles that return different echoes when they bounce off nearby objects. The dolphins recognize the particular patterns produced by shoals of fish as potential food. Inside their distinctive bulging forehead is a lens-shaped wad of fat called the 'melon' that it is thought is used to focus these noises.

♂♀ **Common Genet** *Genetta genetta*

Also known as the Small-spotted Genet, this was once the most widespread genet but it has been hunted for its attractive spotted fur and exterminated locally because it raids domestic poultry. The Common Genet occurs in south-west Europe, north-west Africa and savanna areas south of the Sahara, as well as in southern Arabia. Within this range the solitary, carnivorous Genet inhabits a range of habitats and each night preys on rodents, birds and reptiles. It is an agile climber and can move noiselessly on the ground. The Genet makes its home in an abandoned burrow, hollow tree or among rocks where, after mating, 2–3 young are born. They grow to 50–60cm (19.7–23.6in) with tails of 40–48cm (15.76–18.9in). Genets are reputedly easily tamed and were frequently kept in ancient Egypt to control rats and mice.

♂♀ **Common Hamster** *Cricetus cricetus*

The Common Hamster is a solitary, nocturnal rodent that is to be found on the steppes and farmlands of Europe and western Asia at elevations of less than 500m (about 1640ft). Each adult lives in a burrow, about 2m (6.6ft) deep, which includes separate nesting, latrine and food storage chambers where it often hoards up to 90kg (over 198lb) of food. The Common Hamster also eats some animal matter, as well as grain, roots and vegetables, which it transports to its store in its capacious cheek pouches. From October–March it hibernates, waking occasionally to feed. It is 20–30cm (7.9–11.8in) in length with a 4–6cm (1.6–2.4in) tail. The Common Hamster is a prolific breeder, producing 2 litters of 4–12 young each year.

♂♀ **Common Long-eared Bat**
Plecotus auritus

This bat derives its name from its most conspicuous feature – its enormously long ears that are up to three-quarters as long as its entire body of 5cm (nearly 2in), excluding its tail of about 4cm (1.5in). The ears are normally folded back and relatively inconspicuous when the bat is at rest. The Long-eared Bat has a wingspan of up to 28cm (11in). It ranges from western Europe as far east as Japan – anywhere, in fact, where it finds its principal food of night-flying Noctuid moths which it either catches in flight or else hovers to pick off walls or leaves. Colonies of Long-eared Bats roost in crevices in trees and rocks and often breed in the roofs of houses after which the females give birth to a single young.

♂♀ **Common Pipistrelle**
Pipistrellus pipistrellus

This is the smallest and most common European bat but its range also extends to North Africa and east as far as Kashmir, India. It is a member of the Vespertilionidae or 'Whispering Bat' family and is usually active before any others when it feeds on flying insects. During the day it roosts in lofts, farm buildings or church spires in large groups that frequently number over 1000. In winter it hibernates, sometimes in groups 100 times this size. It mates before hibernation and the sperm is stored inside the female until fertilization occurs the following year. Between 1–2 young are born in June. Common Pipistrelles have a body length of 33–45 mm (1.3–1.8in) and a wingspan of 18–21cm (7–8.2in).

♂♀ **Common Rabbit or Old World Rabbit**
Oryctolagus cuniculus

The Common Rabbit is one of nature's success stories. It originated in the Iberian Peninsula and north-west Africa but over the last 1000 years it has spread, either by its own efforts or helped by man, into the rest of Europe, New Zealand and Australia. In New Zealand and Australia particularly, unhindered by any natural enemies, it has become a serious pest, denuding grasslands and depriving native species of food. Rabbits live in colonies in many individual burrows, up to 3m (9.8ft) deep called warrens, that may be home to several hundred animals and develop over many generations into extensive networks. In alarm rabbits thump the ground with their hindfeet, which is thought to act as a warning signal to others together with the white underside of their tails, which becomes visible when they are running. They are mainly nocturnal, emerging from their burrows at dusk to feed on succulent plants and grass, often seriously damaging vegetable crops. Rabbits are legendary as prolific breeders and one male (buck) mates with several females (does). Litters of 3–9 young are produced almost every month from January–June in a special 60cm (23.6in) long stop. There is a high predation rate with many rabbits taken by badgers, foxes, weasels, rats, gulls and raptors and by man who has hunted them for their skins and delicately flavoured meat since prehistoric times. Common Rabbits are the ancestors of domestic rabbits and grow to 39–52cm (15.4–20.5in), including their tail.

♂♀ **Common Rat or Brown Rat or Norwegian Rat** *Rattus norvegicus*

This highly adaptable rodent originated in eastern Asia and Japan, but has since followed humans throughout the world, profiting from our food stores. Common Rats are among the most serious pests, killing poultry and game and destroying or spoiling crops and grain. Worse still, they are serious carriers of many diseases and are responsible for spreading salmonella and bubonic plague. Incredibly fecund, they produce up to 7 litters of 6–22 young each year throughout their lifespan of 2–4 years. They are omnivorous and good climbers and swimmers able to gnaw their way into places inaccessible to other animals. They have body lengths of 19–27cm (7.5–10.6in) and tails of 13–23cm (5.1–9in). They are aggressive with highly developed senses.

♂♀ **Common Seal or Harbour Seal**
Phoca vitulina

These animals inhabit shallow, northern, sub-Arctic coastal waters and estuaries and are often to be seen in colonies of up to 100, basking on beaches, sand bars and rocks. The females are smaller than the males, which can be as long as 2m (6.6ft). Breeding takes place in midsummer and the cows each give birth to a single pup that can swim and dive almost at once. The main diet of Common Seals is fish, crustaceans and squid. They can stay submerged for 30 minutes reaching depths of up to 100m (328ft), though shallower dives of shorter duration are the norm.

♂♀ **Common Zebra or Burchell's Zebra**
Equus burchelli

The 3 species of zebra are instantly recognizable by their bold stripes that act as disruptive camouflage. The stripes of Common Zebras are the broadest and most widely spaced.

Their colouring is clinal and the southern populations have a yellowish background colour with paler stripes towards their rear. They are distributed on the open plains and lightly wooded savannas of East and South Africa in family groups that typically consist of a mature male (stallion), up to 6 females (mares) and their young (foals). Young males form bachelor herds and old males, which are replaced by younger stallions of 6–8 years old when they are 16–18, live alone. Zebras are diurnal and are often to be found in mixed herds with antelopes. They feed mainly on grass and visit waterholes daily as they need to drink regularly. Their main enemies are the lion, hyaena and hunting dog; the foals also fall prey to leopards and cheetahs and it is thought that only half of the young survive to adulthood. In the mating season rival stallions wrestle each other with their necks followed by more serious fighting to copulate with mares. A single foal is born. Adult Common Zebras grow to 1.9–2.4m (6.2–7.9ft); the mares are smaller.

♂♀ Cougar or Mountain Lion or Puma
Felis concolor

This large, powerful cat is the second largest New World cat after the Jaguar *Panthera onca*. It is distributed from British Columbia south to Patagonia in a wide variety of habitats, such as mountains, jungle, plains, swamps and desert well away from man, who has persistently persecuted it. It is now protected in North America where it is rare. Cougars are solitary carnivores and occupy a territory of up to 200km square (124 miles square) where they prey on birds, hares, rabbits, small mammals and especially deer, which form up to 75 per cent of their diet. They also occasionally take livestock. The northern populations are paler and larger than those in the south and reach a length of 2.5m (over 8ft), including the tail. The southern animals breed throughout the year but in the north 2–4 cubs are born in the summer. Puma cults were an important aspect of the religion of the Andean civilizations for more than 1000 years.

♂♀ Coyote or Prairie Wolf *Canis latrans*

The Coyote used to live mostly in western North America but, despite the slaughter of up to 125,000 each year, in the past century it has spread east to the Atlantic seaboard, north to Alaska and south to Costa Rica and it has even moved into suburban environments. In the New World it has the same reputation for cunning and wariness enjoyed by the red fox in the Old World and it enjoys a central position in the myths and legends of the native North Americans. These largely nocturnal carnivores make a meal of almost anything available, such as insects, fish, snakes, frogs, birds, small mammals of every kind and carrion as well as plant matter. Larger, swifter prey is pursued to exhaustion by members of a pack in relays at speeds of up to 65km/h (over 40mph). Coyotes also play 'dead' and, when a carrion-feeding bird comes to investigate, the shamming animals seize and devour it. They are preyed on in their turn by eagles, wolves and cougars. Coyotes pair for life,

mating in late winter, and 5–10 young are born in a burrow, which is kept scrupulously clean. They grow to 1–1.3m (3.3–4.3ft) long, including their 30–40cm (11.8–15.8in) tail. They are smaller than wolves. The noise of them barking and howling is *de rigueur* for the soundtrack of any Western movie.

♂♀ Cusimanse *Crossarchus obscurus*

The Cusimanse is a mongoose that lives in the tropical rainforests of West Africa from Gambia and Sierra Leone to Ghana up to elevations of 2000m (6562ft). It lives in groups of as many as 12 and searches the forest floor for all kinds of food, including worms, insects, spiders, molluscs, land crabs, frogs, reptiles, small vertebrates and birds and their eggs. It breaks these eggs by throwing them backwards and smashing them against a hard surface such as a rock or tree. Like most mongooses, it also eats venomous snakes that it kills after outmanoeuvring them with its superior agility. It is diurnal and largely terrestrial but climbs trees to escape from an enemy, such as one of the large carnivores. At night it digs a burrow in an old termite hill or similar place. There is no distinct breeding season but a litter of (usually) 4 young are produced about 3 times each year. The Cusimanse grows to a length of 30–40cm (11.8–15.8in) with a tail of 15–25cm (5.9–9.9in).

♂♀ De Brazza's Monkey or Chestnut-browed Guenon *Cercopithecus neglectus*

The swampy and tropical rainforest of Central Africa at altitudes of up to 2000m (6562ft) is the home of De Brazza's Monkeys, named after the Italian-born French explorer, Pierre-Paul de Brazza (1852–1905), who founded the French Congo. They normally live in groups of 15–20, but exceptionally large troops of as many as 200 are reported. They are active in the daytime and feed mainly on the ground. Although they raid plantations, their natural diet is fruit, berries, shoots and leaves and they also eat lizards, insects and birds' eggs. Both sexes have the distinctive beard, but the males are larger than the females and grow to a maximum length of 145cm (57.1in), including a long tail of 85cm (33.5in). Breeding does not seem to be seasonal and a single young is born. Their main predators are leopards, golden cats, eagles and pythons.

♂♀ Dibatag or Clarke's Gazelle
Ammodorcas clarkei

When running this antelope holds its tail erect, which gives it its common name, from the Somali *dabu* meaning 'tail' and *tag* 'erect'. The forward-curving horns are only present in the male, which grows to 1.5–1.6m (4.9–5.2ft) with the famous tail measuring 30–36cm (11.8–14.2in). Dibatags are nomadic and distributed in Ethiopia and Somalia where they live on the semi-arid plains in small groups of up to 6 and their young. Today their range is much reduced due to the depredations of poachers and competition from domestic livestock for their

principal food of leaves, shoots, flowers and grass. They sometimes stand on their hindlegs to reach high into bushes to feed. The breeding period seems to coincide with the rainy season of March–May and a single young is produced once or twice a year. Dibatags have many enemies such as large cats, hyaenas and hunting dogs. Their young are also taken by eagles and ratels.

♂♀ Domestic Cat: Chocolate Burmese
Felis catus

The cat has been domesticated for several thousand years. This breed was reputedly owned by the Burmese aristocracy and each cat was given its own servant. Together with the Siamese and Birman, it was supposedly the traditional sacred cat that guarded Buddhist temples. Today the Burmese is one of the most popular breeds and variations on the original colour brown, such as blue, lilac (or platinum), red, cream, tortoiseshell and chocolate (or champagne) have been bred only since the 1950s. Burmese cats are about 71cm (almost 28in) long, including their tail. From December–August 2–8 blind and deaf kittens are born, which are a 'café au lait' colour that gradually darkens to a rich, chocolate brown. In the wild, cats are stealthy, nocturnal hunters. In the Middle Ages they were often popularly associated with witchcraft and as a result suffered terrible persecutions. This supernatural association probably dates back to ancient Egypt where cats were venerated and, at their death, mummified and entombed.

♂♀ Domestic Cat: Seal Point Siamese
Felis catus

The Siamese Cat shares many characteristics in terms of size and reproduction with the Burmese (see above) but is much more vocal and is thought more aloof. It originated in Siam – modern day Thailand – and is born white or creamy-coloured, only later developing the darker areas or 'points' on its ears, face, legs and tail that designate its type. Apart from the seal point, there are blue point, chocolate point, lilac (or lavender) point, red point, and tabby (or lynx) point varieties. Siamese are also characterized by their blue eyes which, it is said, were a gift from the Buddha for guarding his temples.

♂♀ Domestic Cattle *Bos taurus*

Present-day western Domestic Cattle are descended from the Eurasian Aurochs *B. primigenius*, a wild ox that stood nearly 2m (6.6ft) at the shoulder and became extinct in 1627. Cattle were already domesticated 4500 years ago and over the centuries they have been bred for special characteristics so that today they are divided into dairy, beef and dual-purpose varieties. Cattle are ruminants with complex, 4-chambered stomachs, in which food is broken down by micro-organisms. They periodically bring up food from the first of these chambers to chew the cud. Stature

There is a couple on a flying visit and some animals
you have seen before. It is not only the balloons that are inflated here;
but do seek out a different kind of tiger, a chromatic inaccuracy,
a celestial carnivore and two emblematic beasts.
These snails become harder to find all the time.

and gestation periods to produce a single calf differ between the various breeds. Cattle are a source of leather and, in some societies, fuel and building materials in the form of dung. The Masai of East Africa, whose wealth is measured in cattle, regularly drink the blood of their animals. Much symbolism surrounds cattle and males (bulls), females (cows) and their young (calves) appear in many religions throughout the world. To the Druids, the bull represented the sun and the cow the earth. In ancient Egypt the goddess of the sky, joy and love, Hathor, was depicted with the head of the cow. The cow is also sacred to Hindus.

♂♀ Domestic Dog: Basset Hound
Canis familiaris

Although often kept as a pet, the Basset Hound is a hunting dog with a keen sense of smell (reputedly) second only to that of the bloodhound. It originated in France where it was bred by the nobility to hunt hares and was traditionally followed on foot. The modern breed was developed from a litter introduced into Britain from France by Lord Onslow in 1872. There is an apparent difference between those Basset Hounds that are today kept for hunting, which have longer, straighter legs and fewer wrinkles than those bred for show. The height of a typical dog is 33–38cm (13–15in), but surprisingly these small but compact animals can weigh up to 25kg (over 55lb). The female (bitch), as with all dogs, bears up to 12 blind and deaf young (pups), which are weaned at 4–8 weeks. The dog is often symbolized as faithful, watchful and noble. In ancient Greek myth Cerberus, the 3-headed dog, guarded the threshold to the underworld and the Norse god Odin was counselled by his dogs. The great Mesopotamian goddess of love and war, Ishtar, was sometimes represented as a whelping bitch and in ancient China eclipses were thought to be caused by a celestial mad dog. In medieval Europe dogs, along with cats, were thought to be the forms that witches took when rain-making, which is where we get the modern English expression for heavy rain of 'raining cats and dogs'.

♂♀ Domestic Dog: Beagle *Canis familiaris*

The Beagle hound, as well as being a popular pet, is also a hunting dog used in the pursuit of hares and rabbits. The breed originated in Britain more than 500 years ago and had two distinct sizes – the small 'pocket' Beagles and the larger, so-called 'vaches', which are the animals known today. The height of these animals to the shoulder is between 33–40.5cm (13–16in), though various standards exist for show dogs in different countries.

♂♀ Domestic Dog: Boston Terrier
Canis familiaris

As its name suggests, this breed of dog was developed in the Boston area of New England and is one of the few breeds to have originated in the USA. Popular legend has it that the

coachmen of that region crossed their own dogs – no doubt surreptitiously – with the pedigree dogs of their wealthy employers to create this new breed, which was at first called the Round Head. It would seem evident that the bulldog and the English terrier were among the original ingredients and in 1893 the American Kennel Club recognized this dog as purebred. These animals make affectionate pets and measure 35.5–43cm (about 14–17in) to the shoulder.

♂♀ Domestic Dog: Bull Mastiff
Canis familiaris

In the past many a poacher would have had just cause to fear this powerful beast as it is the traditional gamekeeper's dog bred specifically to outrun and pull down even the fastest and strongest of men. Originally called a Night Dog it only became recognized as a distinct breed in 1924. Its ancestors were the more ponderous mastiff, the bulldog and possibly some form of terrier, which have resulted in a strong, stealthy animal with a pronounced guarding instinct. Bullmastiff dogs are up to 68.5cm tall (almost 27in) at the shoulder.

♂♀ Domestic Dog: Irish Setter
Canis familiaris

The ancestor of the 3 modern breeds of Setter was the so-called Setting Spaniel of medieval times, which was trained to find birds and then 'set' or lie down so that the hunter could throw a net over both the birds and the dog. The modern-day descendants of this dog are the English, Gordon and Irish or Red Setters, which were bred as gundogs and used to quarter the ground ahead of the guns and point (to) the game. The Irish Setter was probably bred from the other two breeds with the addition of some pointer and spaniel, which has resulted in a handsome, good-tempered dog with a distinctive mahogany-coloured coat. The height of a typical Irish Setter is 64–69cm (25–27in).

♂♀ Domestic Dog: Pembroke Welsh Corgi
Canis familiaris

Originally, this was a hardy, working dog known locally as a 'heeler' whose job it was to nip at the heels of cattle to keep the herd moving. Being low on the ground and agile it was able to dodge the hooves. It is thought to have been introduced to Wales from Holland by Flemish weavers in the twelfth century. Nowadays it is a popular pet and a great favourite with the British Royal Family. The ancestor of the modern Pembroke Welsh Corgi was probably a type of spitz and it shares characteristics with the keeshond, samoyed and pomeranian breeds. It has a medium-length coat with a hard texture and short legs. It grows to a height of 25.5–30.4cm (10–12in).

♂♀ Domestic Dog: Pug *Canis familiaris*

The Pug was introduced into England by Dutch traders in the seventeenth century and, like the Pembroke Welsh corgi, it was

favoured by another Royal family, this time the Dutch. Its illustrious associations continue as it is said that the French Empress Josephine used her pet Pug to carry secret messages to her husband Napoleon Bonaparte when he was first imprisoned by the British on Elba. The Pug also deserves a minor footnote in the history of art as 'Trump', the often painted pet of the English artist William Hogarth (1697–1764). This toy dog originated in China where it has been popular for over 2000 years. It probably first reached Holland in a ship of the Dutch East India Company when the trade routes with the Orient were opened up. Pugs, with their tightly curled tails, stand 25.5–28cm (10–11in) at the shoulder.

♂♀ Domestic Dog: Rhodesian Ridgeback
Canis familiaris

The Rhodesian Ridgeback is named for the pronounced ridge of hair growing forwards against the direction of the nap on the rest of its short-haired coat along its spine. It was developed by Boer farmers from dogs brought by the European settlers to South Africa in the sixteenth and seventeenth centuries when crossed with the native Hottentot hunting dogs into a hunting hound. It was introduced into Rhodesia – present-day Zimbabwe – in 1877 to hunt lions and was formerly known as the African Lion Hound. It is a swift, strong dog with great endurance that grows to a maximum height of 68.5cm (nearly 27in).

♂♀ Domestic Dog: Rottweiler
Canis familiaris

When the Roman legions were on the march they were accompanied by herds of cattle that sustained them. These herds were driven and guarded by dogs, some of which were left behind after the fall of the empire at the Roman settlement near Rottweil in present-day Germany. The dog that bears its name would later accompany butchers to and from the town to buy cattle with its master's money secured in a pouch attached to its neck. Whether or not this story is apocryphal, this powerful, forbidding dog would have been a potent deterrent to would-be robbers and today the Rottweiler is still much used as a guard and police dog. It is a stocky, strong and courageous dog that has a reputation for being difficult to control and stands 56–69cm (22–27.2in) high.

♂♀ Domestic Dog: Scottish Terrier
Canis familiaris

The Scottish Terrier retains many of the terrier's original hunting instincts, but does not seem particularly suited to the hunting of game on the Scottish hills for which it was originally bred. Popularly known as the 'Scottie', the whiskers of this dog give it the perpetual air of an old man. Held by many to be the oldest breed of the Highland terriers in the past the name has been used for several similar breeds originating there. Scottish Terriers grow to a maximum height of 25.5m (10in).

Domestic Dog: Shetland Sheepdog
Canis familiaris

The peculiarity that the domestic animals of the Shetland Isles – Shetland ponies, Shetland sheep and Shetland sheepdogs – share is their small size. This is no doubt a result of the harsh and windswept climate of their isolated home off the north coast of Scotland. Although these dogs, which stand 33–41cm (13–16.15in) at the shoulder, look like miniature rough collies the two breeds are unrelated. Shetland Sheepdogs, also known as 'Shelties', are descended from an ancient type of working dog but only became recognized as a distinct breed in 1914. Like all sheepdogs they have excellent guarding instincts.

Domestic Dog: Welsh Springer Spaniel
Canis familiaris

The Spaniel is a gundog bred to flush game from cover into the sights of the waiting hunter's gun and then to retrieve it. The Spaniel is first recorded in Spain, from where it gets its name. Originally known as the 'starter', the Welsh Springer Spaniel is one of the oldest breeds of spaniel. Its coat is always white, slashed with deep red patches. It is a hardy, tireless dog suited to the cold, wet climate and rough terrain of its native Welsh hills. The show standard for this attractive dog is a maximum height of 48.2cm (about 19in).

Domestic Goat *Capra hircus*

Worldwide, goats account for 15 per cent of all domestic grazing animals. They are better able than sheep to digest tough fibre and happily feed on plants considered inedible by other livestock. This is possibly due to the protistans present in their gut that pre-digest cellulose. In the eighteenth century the British Royal Navy adopted a policy of deliberately putting goats ashore on deserted oceanic islands to breed for the benefit of possible shipwrecks. But left to their own devices, goats are tremendously destructive and this misguided altruism resulted in many hitherto lush, paradisiacal habitats becoming completely denuded and the soil eroded. All Domestic Goats are descended from the Asian Pasang *C. aegagrus*; they have been domesticated for more than 8000 years, principally in the more arid regions of the East. Although there is variation among the different breeds, usually 1–2 young (kids) are born. The strong characteristic smell is produced by glands on the head and neck of the male (ram, buck or billy). In some parts of the world goat's meat is eaten, but goats are more usually exploited for the milk (and cheese) from the female (doe or nanny) and for their hides, of which kid leather is especially valuable. Breeds such as the long-haired angora and Kashmir provide valuable superfine, silky hair that is woven into cloth to make high-priced garments. A Domestic Goat grows to about 137cm (almost 54in) long.

Domestic Horse *Equus caballus*

Eohippus – the far distant ancestor of the horse – originated in North America during the Eocene era (about 50 million years ago) and was a small, fox-like animal. *Eohippus*, or the 'dawn-horse', later vanished from that continent but the species continued to evolve through *Orohippus*, *Protohippus* and *Hipparion* into *E. caballus*, the modern horse. It was probably first domesticated about 4000 years ago by the Indo-European tribes who lived on the steppes to the north of the Caspian and Black Seas and has since been developed into many breeds. A 'hand' – originally the breadth of a palm – is the standard unit of measurement for horses and is 4in (roughly 10cm). The stature of the Domestic Horse varies greatly with its breed. A thoroughbred averages 16.1–16.2 hands (64.4–64.8in or about 163cm), a Shire is more massively built and stands 17–18 hands (68–72 in or about 173–185cm) and a Dartmoor pony up to 12.2 hands (48.8in or about 124cm). *See also* Przewalski's Horse. More than any other animal, the horse has influenced the history of mankind. The great invasions of the Mongols and the Moors could only have been accomplished with the aid of the horse; likewise their expulsions. The Native Americans were no match for Cortés (1485–1547) and his mounted conquistadores who, unknowingly, reintroduced the horse to its birthplace.

Domestic Pig or Swine or Hog
(family – *Suidae*)

The ancestor of the modern Domestic Pig was the Wild Boar *Sus scrofa*. It is believed that the pig was first domesticated in eastern Asia about 5000 years ago and today the more than 300 breeds are an important human food source. Pigs are omnivorous scavengers and foragers. A female (sow) can produce 1.5 litters – each averaging 7 piglets – a year. The flesh of the pig is forbidden to followers of certain religions such as Islam and Judaism. Pigs are also a valuable source of fine leather and their bristles – known as hogshair – are used to make high quality paintbrushes, such as the ones used to paint parts of the painting reproduced in this book. *See also* Wild Boar.

Domestic Sheep *Ovis aries*

Today there are approximately a thousand million Domestic Sheep divided into about 450 breeds that are raised principally for their meat, fleeces and milk, which is often made into cheese. They were first domesticated in south-west Asia about 8000 years ago from the Asiatic Mouflon *O. orientalis*. Domestic Sheep have adapted to a wide range of habitats from the wide open spaces of Australia and South America to the bleak mountainsides of Wales where they feed on their principal food, grass. This grazing also restores fertility to depleted land. Humans have exploited sheep's instincts to cluster and they are often herded with the help of trained sheepdogs. Male sheep are called rams, females ewes and the young lambs, which are born in the spring and suckled for about 6 weeks. The lamb especially is the Christian symbol of innocence.

Douc Langur *Pygathrix nemaeus*

The habitat of this monkey suffered terribly in the Indo-China Wars (1946–54 and c.1960–75) that were fought in Vietnam and Laos when countless tonnes of bombs and defoliants were employed. It was also hunted as meat by the guerrilla armies and consequently is now listed as an endangered species. Douc Langurs are diurnal and nomadic, wandering in family groups in the humid forests and forest margins at altitudes of up to 2000m (6562ft) where they feed on leaves, shoots, flowers and fruit, occasionally supplemented with insects and molluscs. They are good swimmers and regularly bathe but little more is known of their habits in the wild. A single young is born that initially clings to its mother's fur. Adult Douc Langurs grow to 150cm (59.1in) long, half of which is their tail. Juvenile males form bands of their own while old males are solitary.

Dromedary or One-humped Camel
Camelus dromedarius

Dromedary or Arabian Camels only exist as domesticated animals, though there is a large, introduced feral population in Australia. They originated in India, the Middle East and North Africa. The light, graceful type are valued as riding and racing animals while the more heavily built type are used as beasts of burden and have been exploited for their milk, wool, hides and meat since 4000 BC. Like Bactrian Camels, *C. bactrianus*, they are ideally suited to a harsh desert environment. They have soft, broad feet for walking on sand, nostrils that close and double rows of eyelashes for keeping out windblown sand. They also possess the legendary ability to go without water for long periods and after an extended period without drinking Dromedaries lose up to 27 per cent of their body weight, which they are capable of rapidly regaining in just 10 minutes by drinking more than 104 litres (23 Imp gal or 27 US gal). Their distinctive hump does not store water but fat and also provides protection by absorbing the heat of the sun. The kidneys are important in conserving water as they concentrate urine and additional moisture is absorbed from faeces. In addition to these specializations, the Dromedary autonomically controls its body temperature; this drops at night to 34°C (93.2°F) and only rises slowly during the day to 40°C (104°F), which delays the point at which it needs to sweat to cool itself. Today Dromedaries are found in the deserts and semi-arid plains of the Middle East and North Africa where they browse on grass and other tough vegetation. A single young is born every second year. An adult Dromedary measures 2.2–3.4m (7.2–11.2ft) in length and has a 50cm (19.7in) long tail.

Eastern Chipmunk or Ground Squirrel
Tamias striatus

Although they can climb well, Eastern Chipmunks are mainly terrestrial rodents. They are common in the forests of eastern North America where their natural curiosity often brings them into contact with humans at camping and picnic sites.

A creature with an industrious reputation that just
might have appeared before. There is also a couple on the
wing from a poem by Poe, a Caledonian creature, an
avian scribe with a serpentine appetite,
a red rodent and Queen Kong.
Can you find this book's title? A snail
could lead you there.

Chipmunks have capacious cheek pouches in which they transport acorns, seeds, nuts and berries to their burrows each autumn to sustain them through the winter. A nineteenth-century naturalist estimated that one individual carried a bushel (35.3 litres or 7.7 Imp gal or 9.3 US gal) in 3 days. In northern latitudes they undergo long torpid periods rather than hibernating, but in the south they emerge from their burrows from time to time during the winter. In spring a single litter of 3–8 blind young is born in a nesting chamber at the end of a 3m (9.8ft) long burrow. In the south of their range a second litter often follows in the summer. They grow to an adult size of 13.5–19cm (5.3–7.5in), with a tail of 7.5–11.5cm (nearly 3–4.5in).

♂♀ Eastern Quoll or Native Cat
Dasyurus viverrinus

The Eastern Quoll was fairly common in south-eastern Australia until the 1930s but today it is thought to survive only on Tasmania. This nocturnal marsupial spends the day in a rock pile or hollow log and emerges at night to hunt the forests and open country for rats, mice and insects. It is mainly terrestrial but can climb well and measures 28–45cm (11–17.7in) with a 17–28cm (6.7–11in) tail. Quolls breed from May–August and up to 18 young are born that continue their development in the mother's pouch. The mother is unable to support so many offspring and within 48 hours 10 or more of her young have died. As the remainder grow they clamber about all over the mother's body.

♂♀ Eland *Tragelaphus oryx*

The nomadic Eland is one of the largest living antelopes and is exceeded in size only by the closely related Giant Eland *T. derbianus*. A mature male reaches a length of 3.4m (11.2ft) with a tail of 75cm (29.6in). It weighs as much as 900kg (1985lb) and has horns of 1m (3.3ft). The female is smaller, and also has horns. Its decline began in the 1890s when an epidemic of rinderpest exterminated it in many parts of its range, which today has shrunk to Ethiopia and East and South Africa. Its numbers have since been further reduced by hunting and the spread of agriculture, but it breeds freely and is now slowly recolonizing many areas. It has been domesticated in parts of Africa and Ukraine. Its natural habitats are open plains, savanna and montane forest up to 4500m (17,764ft) where troops of up to 24 animals browse during the day on grass, shoots, foliage, tubers and melons. In July–November a single young is born.

♂♀ Eurasian Badger *Meles meles*

The home of a Eurasian Badger is known as a sett and consists of an extensive system of burrows with many entrances, often the work of several generations. It is occupied by a family group. This elusive, nocturnal animal sleeps here during the day and spends the winter months in semi-hibernation, emerging at intervals. Eurasian Badgers are distributed in woodland and forests throughout the temperate zones from Ireland in the west

to China and Japan in the east. They are the most omnivorous of the weasel family (Mustelidae) feeding on small mammals, frogs, insects, carrion, fruit, nuts and bulbs as well as their preferred diet of earthworms, which they eat in vast quantities. Badgers have a long history of persecution and in the past were pitted against savage dogs – despite their shyness they are ferocious fighters with strong teeth and powerful foreclaws – in gory spectacles that were finally outlawed in England in the 1850s. They were also hunted for their hair, which was used for making shaving brushes. Today Badgers are protected in many countries. Boars and sows mate in the spring, but due to delayed implantation of the embryo, the resulting litter of 2–4 young (cubs) is not born until the following year. They grow to 70–85cm (27.6–33.5in) with tails of 11–18cm (4.3–7in).

♂♀ Eurasian Otter *Lutra lutra*

Otters are Mustelids that have adapted to a semi-aquatic life and are capable of swimming underwater for up to 400m (over 1312ft) without surfacing to breathe. Their nostrils and ears can be closed and the toes of all four feet are webbed, giving them wonderful speed and manoeuvrability in the water where they prey on fish, crustaceans, amphibians, water birds and voles. They are noted for their playfulness. Otters have long been hunted for their valuable fur and persecuted for the depredations they cause to fisheries. They are solitary and nocturnal and live in burrows called 'holts' or 'dens' in riverbanks with underwater entrances. In spring 2–4 blind, toothless young are born. Male Eurasian Otters are called 'dogs', females 'bitches' and the young 'cubs'. They are distributed across the whole of Europe, parts of North Africa and most of Asia to Japan and the Kuril Islands. Eurasian Otters are 55–83cm (21.7–32.7in) long with tails of 30–55cm (11.8–21.7in). The Loch Ness Monster and the Canadian Ogo-pogo are thought by some to be misinterpretations of a bitch and her cubs swimming in line astern.

♂♀ Eurasian Red Squirrel *Sciurus vulgaris*

The Eurasian Red Squirrel is just one of about 260 species of this large rodent and thrives throughout the forests of Eurasia except in England where it has been displaced to a large extent by the introduced Grey Squirrel *S. carolinensis* from North America. The typical body length of an adult is 23cm (9in) to which must be added its bushy tail of 20cm (7.8in). These agile, arboreal animals do not hibernate, but may remain in the nest during severe weather. They feed – chiefly on conifer cones, beech mast and other tree seeds, but they supplement this diet with fruit, mushrooms, insects, birds' eggs and nestlings – before retreating again to their spherical nests (dreys), which are built in a tree. They are diurnal creatures.

♂♀ European Mole *Talpa europaea*

The ridges and molehills that mar an otherwise perfect lawn are the bane of many gardeners. They are the outward evidence of

burrows just beneath the surface and of where the European Mole has been perpetually digging in search of the earthworms, grubs and other invertebrates that are the main element of its diet. These molehills are formed when excavated earth is pushed to the surface; they also act as air-vents to the 3m (9.8ft) deep occupancy burrows. Using its large, powerful foreclaws, a mole is capable of digging 20m (65.6ft) a day. Alternating periods of activity and rest occur throughout the day and night and a mole eats the equivalent of its own body weight each day and also makes stores of earthworms by first paralysing them with a bite to the head. Moles spend almost their entire life of 3–4 years underground and are not blind, as is popularly believed, though their sense of sight is very poor and they only have tiny eyes. Their tactile sense is highly developed and their facial bristles can detect the least vibration. They are to be found in Europe, excluding Ireland, and east to Central Sibera at altitudes of up to 2000m (6562ft) where there is sufficient depth of soil. A single litter of 4–7 young is produced each year that grow to an adult size of 93–16mm (3.6–6.6in), including the tail.

♂♀ European Mouflon *Ovis musimon*

The European Mouflon is descended from early domesticated sheep that were taken to Corsica and Sardinia in the prehistoric period. Some of these sheep escaped into the wild and have lived in the mountains ever since. The wild progenitor of the European Mouflon is the Asiatic Mouflon *O. orientalis*. The males (rams) have large, curled horns but the females (ewes) have very small ones or none at all. Mouflons have also been introduced to other parts of central and southern Europe where they mainly inhabit scrub and open mountainsides. Like goats, Mouflons feed on an extremely wide variety of plant matter including buds, shoots, flowers and grass. They even eat poisonous plants, such as Deadly Nightshade *Atropa belladonna* without apparent ill effects. They are naturally gregarious and form flocks of females and their young; the males form separate flocks. They come together in the mating season when violent fights break out for possession of females. A single young (lamb) is born that grows to an adult size of 110–130cm (43.3–51.2in); the males are larger than the females.

♂♀ Fallow Deer *Dama dama*

Fallow Deer were originally natives of the eastern Mediterranean region and western Asia, but have been distributed across Europe since Roman times. Today they are abundant in zoos and parks and they have been introduced into North and South America, Australasia, South Africa and Madagascar. They feed on grass, leaves, buds and shoots. Male Fallow Deer have 60cm (23.6in) long palmate antlers, which are shed in May and are regrown by September for the rutting season in October–November. A single fawn is born. Bucks are larger than does and their size ranges from 130–160cm (51.2–63in) with tail lengths of 16–19cm (6.3–7.5in); they weigh 45–100kg (99.2 - 220.5lb).

⚤ **Fennec** *Fennecus zerda*

The Fennec is the smallest member of the fox family and it is found in the deserts of North Africa and the Sinai peninsula where the hairy soles of its feet enable it to move freely over the soft sand. It is also found in the Arabian peninsula, but it is rare there. This nocturnal fox feeds on small rodents, lizards, birds and their eggs, fruit, berries and insects, including scorpions. Like most desert dwellers it can go for many days without water. The most distinctive characteristic of the Fennec is its large ears up to 15cm (nearly 6in) long, which endow it with exceptionally acute hearing and also help in cooling. Its body typically measures up to 41cm (over 16in) and its tail 30cm (11.8in). It passes the heat of the day underground in burrows in family groups of up to 10. Fennecs mate for life and the breeding season is from January–March. The female gives birth to a litter of between 2–5 cubs.

⚤ **Fossa** *Cryptoprocta ferox*

The nocturnal Fossa is found only in Madagascar and is the largest native carnivore of that island where it hunts on the ground and among the forest treetops. It preys on birds, lemurs, reptiles and amphibians and also takes domestic poultry and livestock. As a result of hunting and the reduction of their habitat and prey, Fossas are now rare over most of their range. They are solitary except in the breeding season and the female bears 2–3 young in a burrow, hollow tree or rocky lair. The young eventually reach their adult size of about 60–80cm (23.6–31.5in) long with their tails a similar length.

⚤ **Four-toed Elephant Shrew or Jumping Shrew** *Petrodromus tetradactylus*

There are 16 species of Elephant Shrew, which are named for their mobile, elongated, flexible snouts. They are abundant and active by day and night. Four-toed Elephant Shrews are distributed from Natal north to Kenya, Zanzibar and Mafia Island and parts of Zaïre and Angola. They feed on insects, especially ants and termites, which they uncover by scraping the ground with their hindfeet. Their main enemies are snakes, raptors and small carnivores that they attempt to evade by jumping with long leaps. Four-toed Elephant Shrews reproduce throughout the year and a single young is produced in the rainy season. When fully grown they measure 16–22cm (6.3–8.7in) with tails of 13–18cm (5.1–7in). Some mystery surrounds their precise place in the animal kingdom, but they are now classified as a distinct order Macroscelididae.

⚤ **Franquet's Fruit Bat or Epauleted Bat** *Epomops franqueti*

Twenty-five per cent of all mammals are bats, which are the only mammals capable of true flight. About 154 species of these are fruit bats or flying foxes, the largest of which have wingspans of 1.5m (4.9ft). The white patches of fur on their shoulders give Franquet's Fruit Bats their alternative common name and they are distributed in Africa from Zimbabwe and Tanzania west to Nigeria and Angola. They rely on their sense of sight rather than echolocation and feed on fruit. Franquet's Fruit Bats have body lengths of 13.5–18cm (5.3–7in) and wingspans of 23–25cm (9–9.9in). There is no fixed breeding season and a single young is produced.

⚤ **Gemsbok or Fringe-eared Oryx** *Oryx gazella*

Both male and female Gemsboks have horns, of which the larger male's are up to 127cm (50in) long. Gemsboks live on the dry savanna and semi-deserts of western South Africa in herds of 30–40. They form larger migratory herds in the dry season to search for the steppe grass that is their principal diet along with bulbs, tubers, roots and ground fruit such as melons. Old males are solitary. Gemsboks are capable of surviving without drinking for extended periods as they can extract much of their moisture requirements from plant matter. Their principal enemy is humans, but they are also prey to lions, leopards and hunting dogs and the calves are also vulnerable to cheetahs, hyaenas, jackals, caracals and servals. A single calf is born that grows to an adult size of 1.6–2.3m (5.2–7.7ft).

⚤ **Giant Anteater** *Myrmecophaga tridactyla*

The diurnal Giant Anteater has an appropriately large appetite for ants and termites and consumes as many as 30,000 each day, which it collects on its 61cm (24in) long, sticky tongue. Its thick fur protects it both from being bitten and from the low temperatures that can fall below 0°C (32°F) at night in the more mountainous parts of its range, which is from Central America to northern Argentina. It inhabits forests, swamps and open savannas and is a good swimmer. The Giant Anteater is solitary and has large, powerful foreclaws for breaking down termitaria. Apart from humans, its only natural enemy is the jaguar. The single young initially travels about on its mother's back. Including its tail, the Giant Anteater measures up to 1.8m (5.9ft) long.

⚤ **Giant Panda** *Ailuropoda melanoleuca*

The Giant Panda is one of the rarest animals in the world and is found only in the bamboo forests of the Szechwan, Kansu, and Shensi provinces of China. Zoological authorities differ as to its origins some placing it as a relative of the bear and others of the raccoon. The Giant Panda is an elusive, solitary and nocturnal creature that passes the summer at altitudes of 2700–3900m (over 8850–nearly 12,800ft). It spends up to 75 per cent of the day feeding on bamboo, which is virtually the sole component of its diet. It has even evolved a specialized forepaw with which to grasp these bamboo stems. It is believed that the decrease of bamboo, due to long-term climatic changes, is one reason for the decline of this animal. Other major factors in its decline include the expansion of the human population, deforestation and hunting. In January a litter of 1–3 young is born but usually only one survives. Giant Pandas rarely breed successfully in captivity and there are now thought to be no more than 1000 animals surviving in the wild. A fully grown Giant Panda measures 1.5m (4.9ft) with a stubby tail of 12.5cm (4.9in).

⚤ **Giant Pangolin or Scaly Anteater** *Manis gigantea*

The nocturnal Giant Pangolin is a slow, deliberate mover and is often killed in bush fires. It is also hunted for its meat and its scales are sought after as charms. Its range extends from Senegal in the west to Uganda in the east and Angola in the south. It feeds on ants and termites and breaks into termitaria with its strong foreclaws, lapping up the unlucky occupants with its long, sticky tongue. It is capable of swimming and of standing upright using its thick tail to form a tripod. When threatened it rolls itself into a ball, presenting its aggressor with the sharp edges of its large, overlapping scales. It also sprays urine and emits a strong-smelling secretion from an anal gland. The smaller female gives birth to a single offspring in an underground burrow up to 40m (131.2ft) long and 5m (16.4ft) deep. The scales of the newborn are soft but harden over a period of 2 days. It is weaned by 3 months. The larger male measures 80cm (31.5in) with a tail of 65cm (25.6in).

⚤ **Giraffe** *Giraffa camelopardalis*

The Giraffe is the tallest of the mammals, reaching a height of 5.8m (over 19ft) and a weight of up to 1950kg (4299lb). It is believed to once have been present over most of Africa and some unusual rock engravings of it are to be found at Fezzan in south-western Libya in the middle of what is now the Sahara Desert. Today troops of Giraffe live mainly on the savanna of sub-Saharan Africa in groups of up to a dozen. Their long necks allow them to browse among the upper branches of acacia trees and thorn bushes. During the mating season males wrestle each other with their necks for possession of females. Giraffes give birth to (usually) a single young, always at dawn. They possess a remarkable system of valved blood-vessels and alternative routes for blood flow that prevent a rush of blood to the head when they lower it to drink. Early travellers thought the Giraffe was a hybrid creature from the mating of a camel and a leopard – an erroneous belief which is betrayed in its Latin name. To the Arabs and the Chinese the Giraffe is a symbol of peace and gentleness.

⚤ **Gorilla** *Gorilla gorilla*

The Gorilla is the largest of the primates; a male weighs up to 275kg (over 606lb) and measures 1.75m (almost 6ft) when standing erect. In captivity it can grow even larger but the female is smaller and, on average, attains only half the weight of the male. Gorillas are shy, unaggressive vegetarians. Their main food is leaves, ferns, stalks, bamboo and roots that, with their enormous strength, they easily pull up. Gorillas are diurnal

This detail has a particularly shy snail. If you can find it you are just the kind of person who might solve this riddle. There are also the world's longest reptile, a watery dweller in the eighth house, a charming bird, an exploding duck, a high-ranking communist sailor and the unicorn's wife.

and spend most of the day either foraging or resting on the ground, but at dusk they each build a nest of leaves and branches in which to pass the night. All Gorillas are found in the dense forests of equatorial Africa. The Mountain Gorilla *G. gorilla beringei* is an especially endangered subspecies and probably numbers no more than 650 individuals. The older males in a group develop distinctive bony crests on their head and 'saddles' of silver fur on their back and are known as 'silverbacks' while the younger male members are termed 'blackbacks'. Females, juveniles and infants complete the group of 15–40 and are better able to climb trees than the massive males. Gorillas breed at any time of the year and a single baby is born that stays with its mother for 3–4 years.

♂♀ Grant's Gazelle *Gazella granti*

Herds of up to 400 of these large, slender gazelles can be found wandering the savannas and semi-desert areas of equatorial Africa. They browse on grasses and leaves and they may remain in one area for extended periods if sufficient food is available. They seem to satisfy most of their moisture needs from their food and need to visit watering places only irregularly. In the breeding season the size of the herds decreases to about 30 when a male takes charge of a 'harem' of females in rut and drives off prospective rivals. Usually a single calf is produced at any time of the year and is especially vulnerable to predators such as baboons, hyaenas, pythons and eagles. Adult antelopes are also preyed on by lions, leopards, cheetahs and hunting dogs. A mature male Grant's Gazelle is 130–150cm (51.2–59.1in) long with a 25–35cm (9.8–13.8in) tail; the female is smaller. The female has horns about half the size of the male's which can measure 80cm (31.5in).

♂♀ Greater Bushbaby or Thick-tailed Galago *Otolemur crassicaudatus*

The call of this nocturnal animal, which may be made up to 100 times each hour in the early evening, sounds like that of a child, hence its common name 'Bushbaby'. Greater Bushbabies are distributed in forests and wooded savannas and at altitudes of up to 3500m (11,483ft) from Somalia and Kenya to South Africa where they lead a mainly arboreal existence. Some plant matter is eaten, but mainly birds and their eggs, reptiles and insects. By day Bushbabies sleep concealed in dense foliage or in hollow trees and their principal enemies are snakes, genets and owls. Between May–October a litter of 1–3 young is born. Greater Bushbabies are about the size of rabbits and measure 60–99cm (23.6–39in), including their long tails.

♂♀ Greater Kudu *Tragelaphus strepsiceros*

The males (bulls) of this species of large, beautiful antelope were once extensively hunted, chiefly for their elegant, corkscrew horns that are held flat along their back when running. It is presumed that the smaller and normally hornless females (cows) did not suffer a similar fate. Greater Kudus live in the dry, rocky and scrub country of eastern and southern Africa where they browse on leaves, shoots and seeds, occasionally raiding crops that they are capable of reaching even by leaping over 2.5m (8.2ft) high fences. Male Greater Kudus measure up to 2.5m (8ft) with tails of 55cm (over 21in) and horns as long as 1m (3.3ft). A single calf is produced. These antelopes have recently been reintroduced to the Transvaal and were introduced into New Mexico in 1962 where they are thriving.

♂♀ Great Jerboa *Allactaga major*

The locomotion of the Great Jerboa is similar to that of the kangaroo as it leaps about on its hindlegs, which can be 4 times longer than its forelimbs, and uses its long tail as a counterbalance. In flight a single leap might cover 3m (9.8ft). Great Jerboas are nocturnal and pass their days beneath the ground in a complex system of burrows where they also hibernate in the winter months. Their small, manipulative forelimbs are used for combing the sand of their native semi-desert and steppe habitat, from the Ukraine east to China, in search of insects and seeds. Little information is available about the breeding cycle of these rodents, but 1–2 litters of about 3 young each are produced each year. In adulthood Great Jerboas grow to 9–15cm (3.5–5.9in) long with tails of 16–22cm (6.3–8.7in).

♂♀ Guereza or Eastern Black and White Colobus *Colobus guereza*

The hunting of this monkey for its beautiful pelt has led to its extinction in most of East Africa. Millions of skins were exported in the last century to satisfy the European fur trade and hundreds of thousands are still taken annually today. The diurnal Guereza is distributed in the Congo and Zaïre, but its numbers are declining in Uganda, Cameroon, Sudan and Ethiopia due to hunting and the spread of agriculture. Guerezas have evolved complex stomachs to cope with their vegetarian diet, which they find in the forest canopy. Thumbless, they are wonderfully agile and leap from tree to tree often using springy branches to catapult themselves. Eagles are their principal enemy. There is no fixed breeding season and a single young is born. It is completely white, but gradually achieves adult colouring. It eventually grows to 48–70cm (18.9–27.6in) with a tail of 67–90cm (26.4–35.5in). The males are larger than the females.

♂♀ Hedgehog *Erinaceus europaeus*

Their habit of rooting around in hedgerows while making noisy stamping, grunting and snuffling sounds earns these familiar European mammals their common name. Hedgehogs are distributed throughout western Europe from the British Isles to Scandinavia and east to Romania and at altitudes of up to 2000m (6562ft) in the Alps. They are most often found near woodland and in grassland. They eat a wide range of foods, including insects, earthworms, molluscs, small vertebrates, reptiles, birds' eggs and nestlings. When threatened they roll themselves up into tight balls, presenting their aggressor with an array of sharp spines. Hedgehogs are solitary and nocturnal and, as they are slow movers, they frequently fall victim to cars when crossing roads. Those in the north of the range hibernate from October–April in a nest made from dry leaves, usually beneath a dense shrub or outbuilding. While in a state of hibernation their body temperature falls to that of their surroundings, their heart rate to about 20 beats per minute and their respiration to 10 breaths per minute. Between 1–2 litters of 3–10 blind, soft-spined young are produced each year. Adult Hedgehogs measure 13.5–27cm (5.3–10.6in) with short tails of 1–5cm (0.4–2in).

♂♀ Himalayan Tahr *Hemitragus jemlahicus*

The goat-like Himalayan Tahr lives in herds of 30–40 and is at home below the tree line on the perilously steep mountainsides of northern India, Nepal and Sikkim. It was introduced to New Zealand in 1904 and to South Africa in 1930. The species is now under threat in its homeland from overhunting for its meat and hide. It feeds on grass and other plant matter and fruit. Both sexes have thick, backward-curving horns. The males have manes on the neck, shoulders and breast and are larger than the females. They measure 150–175cm (59.1–68.9in) with tails of 15–20cm (5.9–7.9in). The rut is in November–December when the males give off a strong, characteristic odour from an anal gland. The female gives birth to a single young that is soon agile and joins the herd when just a few hours old.

♂♀ Hippopotamus *Hippopotamus amphibius*

The name Hippopotamus is Greek for 'horse of the river', which is where it spends most of its time in order to support its vast bulk of up to 4500kg (9922lb). Hippopotamuses range from the Upper Nile Valley in northern Africa to Namibia and parts of South Africa. These giant vegetarians are sociable creatures that live in groups of 15 or so, though they are sometimes aggressive and are known to be responsible for a number of human deaths each year. The glandular skin of the Hippopotamus secretes a red pigmented mucus that protects it from the sun and water and once gave rise to the belief that the animal sweated blood. In ancient Egyptian theology the goddess Taueret (also called Apet or Opet) was represented with the head of a Hippopotamus and was worshipped as the goddess of childbirth.

♂♀ Honey Possum *Tarsipes rostratus*

The marsupial Honey Possum is the sole member of the family Tarsipedidae with no close relatives. It lives in the heathlands of south-western Australia. It feeds almost solely on the pollen and nectar of the flowers of the banksia, callistemon and eucalyptus plants, which are only found there. But as a result of creeping urbanization, these plants, and thus the Honey Possum, are under threat. The Honey Possum collects the nectar and pollen on the bristly tip of its 2.5cm (nearly 1in) long tongue, which is rather like that of the hummingbird, and scrapes it off against its ridged palate. The mating season is in midwinter and 2 young are produced that stay in their mother's pouch for about 4 months. Honey Possums are 7–8.5cm (2.8–3.3in) long and have 9–10cm (3.5–3.9in) long prehensile tails with which they often hang upside down when feeding.

♂♀ House Mouse *Mus musculus*

Its commensal association with man has turned the House Mouse into one of the most successful mammal species and, though originally a native of the grassy steppes of Asia and eastern Europe, it has now spread to all the populated parts of the earth, even inhabiting such unlikely places as mines and cooling plants. It often takes up residence in a house wall, floor or roof cavity and can be extremely destructive. The House Mouse even feeds off substances inedible to other creatures such as soap, glue and paste. It spoils much more than it consumes. The House Mouse is also responsible for transmitting diseases dangerous to humans, such as salmonella and murine typhus. It makes a well-hidden nest of gnawed scraps of rag, paper, straw or the stuffing from furniture from where it ventures forth on nocturnal foraging trips. When conditions are right, House Mice are prolific breeders. They become sexually mature at 5–7 weeks and breed throughout the year producing a litter of up to 12 young in 3 weeks. A fully grown adult measures 73–102mm (2.8–4in) with a tail of 67–95mm (2.6–3.7in).

♂♀ Human *Homo sapiens*

There is evidence to suggest that modern man – *Homo sapiens* – evolved from his immediate ancestor *Homo erectus* perhaps as long as 350,000 years ago. There are distinct racial differences – particularly in skin colour and stature – and wide variation among individuals and an average adult Caucasian man, for example, measures 1.75m (5.7ft) and an average woman 1.6m (5.3ft) tall. Among the greatest documented physical extremes for adult Humans are: maximum height, 2.7m (nearly 9ft), minimum height 59cm (23.2in); maximum weight 583kg (1187lb), minimum weight 2.12kg (4.2lb). Each of these cases is exceptional. Humans are omnivorous, supremely adaptable creatures and are to be found living in the widest range of habitats from the frigid Arctic regions to scorching tropical and desert environments. Humans are able to mate at any season and the woman usually gives birth to a single child, which stays with its parents for many years.

♂♀ Hunting Dog or Painted Dog *Lycaon pictus*

The nomadic Hunting Dog is highly social and lives and hunts in packs of 15, led by a dominant male and a dominant female. It inhabits plains, savannas and semi-desert at altitudes of up to 3000m (9843ft) over ever decreasing parts of sub-Saharan Africa. Its prey is often much larger than it is and includes antelopes, zebras and even wildebeest. The prey is killed following a chase by the pack, which has great stamina and can

run at 50km/h (over 31mph) for more than 5km (over 3 miles) and sprint at up to 66km/h (nearly 41mph). The disgorged meat is fed to members of the pack that remained behind guarding the young. The number of Hunting Dogs has declined greatly and it was thought that by 1980 there were fewer than 7000 animals in the wild due to the reduction in the numbers of their prey, disease and persecution by man. Mating takes place in late winter and a litter of (usually) 5–7 young is born blind in a burrow abandoned by an aardvark or warthog. Hunting Dogs are 80–108cm (31.5–42.6in) long, with tails of 30–40cm (11.8-15.8in).

♂♀ Ibex *Capra ibex*

The Ibex is a wild goat that lives above the tree line on the high mountains of Europe, Central Asia, Siberia, North Africa, Arabia and the Himalayas at altitudes of up to 6700m (over 21,982ft). It feeds on grass, shrubs and alpine vegetation. The Ibex lives in small herds of females and their young while the older males form separate herds, coming together only in the winter rutting season when the males fight with their long, curved horns to establish rank within the group. A single young is born in spring and is able to follow its mother on the precipitous slopes after only a few hours. Females have much smaller and more slender horns than those of the male. Ibexes are 1.3–1.6m (4.3–5.2ft) long. They are now protected in Europe as their numbers there declined almost to the point of extinction from overhunting.

♂♀ Indri *Indri indri*

Indris are the largest of the lemurs and grow to 61–90cm (24–35.5in) with short tails of 5–6cm (nearly 2–2.4in). Lemurs are the only primates found on Madagascar and the Comoro Islands, which are thought to have separated from Africa about 65 million years ago before the appearance of the monkeys and apes. Indris can be found in forests at altitudes of up to 1800m (5905ft) and are diurnal and arboreal, living in small groups of 2–5 that feed throughout the day on shoots, fruit, flowers and leaves. Nowadays, though their current range is restricted due to loss of habitat from logging, they are a protected species. They have a loud cry that is audible over distances of up to 2km (1.2 miles) and their principal enemy is the fossa. The mating season is in January–February and a single young is born that initially clings to its mother's underside and later rides on her back.

♂♀ Jaguar *Panthera onca*

This is the biggest New World cat and the larger males grow to 1.5m (5ft) with tails of 75cm (29.55in). Jaguars found in the south are larger than those in the north of their range, which extends from south-western USA to Patagonia. It is thought that 'Jaguar' is derived from the native word *Jaguara*, which is colourfully translated as 'the carnivore that overcomes its prey in a single bound'. Jaguars' favoured habitats are dense forest, swamps and riverine areas, and they are also good swimmers

and eat fish and turtles as well as their preferred diet of peccaries, capybaras, tapirs, deer and monkeys. Jaguars prey on domestic animals too, such as cattle, horses and dogs and this has earned them the enmity of man in many areas. They are normally solitary, coming together briefly only every second year to mate. This takes place towards the end of the year or throughout the year in the tropics when a litter of up to 4 cubs is born. Jaguar cults had a prominent place in the religion of the Olmecs, which flourished in Meso-America in the first millennium BC, and the dominant motif of their art was the Jaguar and a Jaguar-human hybrid.

♂♀ Killer Whale or Orca or Grampus *Orcinus orca*

Killer Whales are distributed in seas worldwide where they hunt in coastal waters in packs of up to 50. They sometimes prey in a highly organized manner on seals, penguins, fish, cephalopods and the young of other species of whale, even occasionally attacking the adults. They can swim at speeds in excess of 45km/h (nearly 28mph) in pursuit of prey. Killer Whales are the largest member of the dolphin family (Delphinidae) and mature adult males measure up to 9.8m (32.2ft) and weigh as much as 9000kg (19,845lb). Males are much larger than females. A single young (calf) measuring 2.4m (about 7.9ft) is produced. Killer Whales feature in many myths of the Native Americans of the Pacific north-west coast and are usually associated with evil magic that must be overcome by a hero.

♂♀ Kinkajou *Potos flavus*

Also sometimes called a 'Honey Bear', the nocturnal Kinkajou is easily tamed and is often kept as a pet by the indigenous population. It lives alone or in pairs and is distributed from eastern Mexico south to Brazil where it inhabits forests. Kinkajous are arboreal and are about 95cm (37.4in) long, including their prehensile tails, from which they often hang while feeding on fruit, small mammals, birds and their eggs, insects and honey. Their thick fur protects them from the stings of the irate bees. A litter of 1 (sometimes 2) young is produced in spring or summer.

♂♀ Koala *Phascolarctos cinereus*

No doubt due to its resemblance to a teddy bear people sometimes think of the Koala as a bear, but, in fact, it is a marsupial and is the sole member of the family Phascolarctidae. It is a nocturnal, arboreal animal that rarely descends to the ground except to move to another tree. It lives in the dry forests of eastern Australia where its diet consists almost exclusively of eucalyptus leaves and bark and it reputedly smells like a cough lozenge. Occasionally, it also eats earth, which it is believed aids its digestion. Koalas live alone or in small groups of females led by a male and a single young is produced in the summer of each alternate year. After it is born, the tiny baby enters its mother's backward-facing pouch where it stays for 6 months. It then

A pair of religious parakeets and a charming chimp.

A travelling insect and a fast car.

Negligent parents and a South African sportsperson.

A musteline status symbol and a Christmas conveyor.

Do not forget to find the snail.

climbs out and clings first on to her stomach and later on to her back where it is weaned on its mother's excreta for six weeks. When fully grown a Koala measures 60–85cm (23.6–33.5in). Koalas were once mercilessly hunted for their skins and several million pelts were exported each year. Today they are protected and are slowly becoming re-established, though the chief dangers to these slow-moving creatures are forest fires and the fatal fungal disease cryptococcosis, which infects the respiratory and central nervous systems and which can be transferred to humans.

♂♀ Kongoni or Hartebeest
Alcelaphus buselaphus

The Kongoni can often be found in mixed herds together with zebra, gazelle and wildebeest on the grassy sub-Saharan plains of Africa. But due to overhunting, disease and the destruction of its habitat it is now rare or extinct in many areas. Certain subspecies are critically endangered. Both sexes have the distinctive lyre-shaped horns that on the males grow to 70cm (27.6in). Kongonis feed on grasses and herbage and, if necessary, can go without water for months. They are preyed on by lions, leopards, cheetahs, hyaenas and hunting dogs and their calves are taken by jackals, servals, caracals, eagles and pythons. A single calf is produced. Kongonis are 1.5–2.5m (4.9–8ft) long and have 30–70cm (11.8-27.6in) tails.

♂♀ Leopard *Panthera pardus*

The Leopard, well known for its attractive spotted coat, also includes melanistic individuals known as Black Panthers. The range includes sub-Saharan Africa, North Africa, Asia Minor, India and Asia as far east as China and Korea. It is considered endangered in the latter regions. Aside from the black individuals, the colouring of the Leopard's coat can vary considerably over this vast range and even includes rare cases of albinism. Leopards can be found in all types of habitat from dense rainforest, deserts, savanna and even up to the snow line in mountainous areas. Males are larger and heavier than females and their size varies greatly; an average male measures 210cm (82.7in) with a tail of 70cm (27.5in), though it can grow much bigger in favourable circumstances. Leopards are solitary, stealthy, nocturnal cats that prey on creatures as diverse as fish, birds, lizards, snakes, and mammals from small rodents to large antelopes. They reputedly have a special appetite for dogs and baboons. Leopards are expert climbers and haul quite large kills into trees for safekeeping. Usually 2–3 cubs are born at any time of the year.

♂♀ Lesser Horseshoe Bat
Rhinolophus hipposideros

Horseshoe Bats are named for the complex, fleshy, horseshoe-shaped 'leaf' that surrounds their nose and which focuses their ultrasonic pulses into a beam with which they detect their prey by echolocation. Their diet consists mainly of low-flying insects.

Lesser Horseshoe Bats are one of the smaller members of the family Rhinolophidae and have body lengths of 37–43mm (1.4–1.7in) and wingspans of 19–22.5cm (7.4–8.8in). They are distributed in the warmer regions of western and southern Europe, North Africa and Asia where they inhabit wooded and open country and they take to the wing about 30 minutes after sunset. During the day they roost in colonies in attics, farm buildings and the like and in winter in damp, dark caves, tunnels and cellars where they hang by their feet from the roof with their wings wrapped around their bodies. A single young is born in the spring. These bats have undergone a massive decline in Europe this century.

♂♀ Lesser Panda or Red Panda *Ailurus fulgens*

The Lesser Panda lives in the mountains of Nepal, northern Burma and south-western China at altitudes above 1525m (5003ft). Related to the raccoon, which it superficially resembles, it is nocturnal and feeds mainly on fruit and plant material supplemented by birds' eggs and insects. It passes the day asleep in the upper branches of trees and lives in small family groups of mother plus young; the males are solitary. A litter of (usually) 1–2 young is born in spring. They grow to a full size of 79–112cm (31.1–44.1in), including their bushy tails.

♂♀ Lion *Panthera leo*

The fabled 'King of the Jungle', in fact, does not live anywhere near the tropical forest but rather inhabits the woodland, semi-desert and dry savanna of sub-Saharan Africa and the Gir Forest in north-west India where it is strictly protected. In prehistoric times it ranged over most of the northern hemisphere and northern South America; it finally became extinct in Europe about 2000 years ago. It is a sociable animal and lives together in groups (prides) that commonly consist of 1–3 males, up to 15 females (Lionesses) and numerous juveniles (cubs), the males of which are driven out of the pride when they become mature at about 18 months old and form roving bachelor groups. Females lack the thick manes and are smaller than the males, which may measure 2.5m (8.2ft) long with a tail of over 1m (3.4ft). Lions seem to be lazy beasts and rest for about 20 hours each day, devoting the remaining time to co-operative hunting – principally antelope and zebra, sometimes buffalo and giraffe and occasionally other small mammals, birds and snakes, as well as feeding on carrion. Man-eating Lions are rare. The loud roar of the male Lion can be heard for up to 8km (nearly 5 miles) and is used to warn off other males from its hunting ground. The Lion is the traditional heraldic beast of England. In the ancient Egyptian religion Sekhmet, the terrible goddess of war, was represented as a Lioness or as a woman with the head of a Lioness.

♂♀ Llama *Lama glama*

Nowadays Llamas exist as domesticated animals only. They have been kept for more than 4000 years primarily as pack

animals and also as a source of meat, wool, hide and tallow; their dung was burnt as fuel. Llamas are found in the Andes of South America at altitudes up to 5000m (16,405ft), which they are ideally suited to as the haemoglobin in their blood can absorb more oxygen than any other mammal. The average Llama stands 120cm (47.3in) at the shoulder and is capable of carrying 45–60kg (99.2–132.3lb) on its back. A single young is born that soon becomes active. The Incas, whose empire was centred on what is now Peru and which flourished from c.1100–1531, sacrificed Llamas; the death of white animals ensured health and black ones, rain. In the equivalent Incan legend to Noah's Ark and the Flood, 'Noah' was warned by a Llama to climb to the top of a mountain where he found two of each of the animals that were to survive and repopulate the Earth.

♂♀ Lynx *Felis lynx*

The solitary, nocturnal Lynx can be distinguished by the tufts of hair on its ears and cheeks. It is distributed in the isolated parts of Europe, Asia and northern North America. It hunts the scrub and coniferous forests for hares, young deer, rodents and ground-living birds and it has legendary senses of sight and hearing. Lynxes are a protected species over much of their range since their numbers have been drastically reduced due to overhunting and loss of habitat to man. Males and females come together to mate in March and a litter of 2–4 kittens is born in a den among rocks or in a hollow tree. Northern Lynxes are larger than those found further south and their adult size ranges accordingly between 80–130cm (31.5–51.2in) with tails of 10–20cm (3.9–7.9in).

♂♀ Malayan Tapir or Asian Tapir
Tapirus indicus

The Malayan or Asian Tapir is distinct from its South American cousins chiefly by its striking markings that become excellent camouflage during the night when it is active. It is a solitary, timid vegetarian that occurs in the swamps and jungles of southern Burma, Thailand, Malaya and Sumatra. An adult Malayan Tapir typically measures 2.4m long (7.9ft). Even though this creature is very rare it is seldom hunted by man in those regions where Islam prevails as its flesh, like that of the pig, is considered unclean by Muslims. Its chief predator is the tiger.

♂♀ Markhor *Capra falconeri*

The spectacular corkscrew horns of the female Markhor are longer than those of the male and reach 1.7m (5.6ft) when measured along the curves. But the bearded male is much larger: it measures 1.9m (over 6ft) long, including the 15cm (5.9in) tail. This diurnal wild goat is distributed in the mountainous regions of Uzbekistan, Tadjikistan, Afghanistan, Pakistan and Kashmir at altitudes of 600–3600m (1968–11,811ft). It lives in small herds comprising females and their young. The normally solitary males join them only in the mating season when they engage in duels for the possession of females. Between 1–2 young are born that soon become agile. Markhors feed on grass, lichen, moss and other plant matter. Their horns are much sought after as hunting trophies and this has contributed to their decline. Today there are probably fewer than 25,000 extant in the wild.

♂♀ Mona Monkey *Cercopithecus mona*

The home of the Mona Monkey is the tropical forests and coastal mangroves of West and Central Africa where it feeds on leaves, shoots and fruit, sometimes raiding plantations. It is diurnal and lives in family troops of 5–18, overseen by an old male, which sometimes associate with troops of Black-cheeked White-nosed Monkeys *C. ascanius*. Mona Monkeys are arboreal and each troop has an established territory, with regular routes and dormitories. Their principal enemies are eagles, pythons and leopards. Mating takes place throughout the year. A single young is born that eventually grows to an adult size of 40–60cm (15.8–23.6in) with a tail of 54–80cm (21.3–31.5in).

♂♀ Moonrat *Echinosorex gynmurus*

There is little information available about the secretive and elusive Moonrat that is indigenous to Cambodia, Thailand, Malaysia, Burma, Sumatra and Borneo where it inhabits forests and mangrove swamps. It is the world's largest insectivore, measuring 26–44cm (10.2–17.3in) with a sparsely haired tail of 20–21cm (7.9–8.3in), but its diet also includes worms, molluscs, fruit, fish and crustaceans. If attacked the Moonrat defends itself by emitting a fetid odour from twin anal glands. It is a solitary and nocturnal member of the hedgehog family (Erinaceidae), but has coarse guard hairs rather than spines. There does not seem to be a fixed breeding season and normally 2 young are produced.

♂♀ Moose or Elk *Alces alces*

Confusingly, in Europe this species is called the Elk while in North America that name is applied to the Wapiti *Cervus canadensis*. The common name Moose is derived from the native Algonquian word *musee*, meaning 'wood-eater'. The females (cows) are hornless but the palmate antlers of the male (bull), which are shed annually, may measure 2m (6.6ft) across and are much prized as hunting trophies. This has pushed their range north and the Moose is now a protected species. The Moose is the largest deer and an Alaskan male can measure 3m (9.8ft) long. It inhabits the northern coniferous forests of Europe and North America, usually near water, and it has been introduced into New Zealand. It feeds on the leaves and twigs of aspen, willow, alder and poplar as well as pine shoots and aquatic vegetation. It is usually solitary outside the autumn breeding season, but at that time the males become unpredictable and bellicose and fight each other to mate with several females. The cow gives birth to 1–2 calves. The young

are vulnerable to wolves, bears, cougars, coyotes and wolverines.

♂♀ Mountain Goat *Oreamnos americanus*

Despite its common name, this creature is not a true goat but is closer to the Chamois *Rupicapra rupicapra* and the Serow *Capricornis sumatraensis*. It inhabits the sheer slopes of the Rocky Mountains of North America above the tree line. It has a long, hairy white coat over a woolly underfur that acts as snow camouflage and adapts it perfectly to this harsh environment. Its hooves have a spongy undersurface that enables it to grip rocks on vertiginous, seemingly inaccessible gradients where it feeds on lichen, moss, grass and sedge. Both sexes have horns and can leap gaps of up to 3.5m (11.5ft) with ease. In winter they form flocks but at other times they are in small family groups of 2–4 and mating takes place in November when males (billies) fight for females (nannies). A single young (kid) is born and can follow its parents after only 30 minutes. Males are larger than females and measure up to 1.6m (5.2ft).

♂♀ Muntjac or Barking Deer *Muntiacus reevesi*

Measuring 80–100cm (31.5–39.3in), the Muntjac is little larger than a fox. It has a loud, barking call, which gives it its alternative common name. The male has small antlers that rarely exceed 15cm (5.9in) long and project from pedicels and tusks formed from the upper canine teeth. They can be used during the rut to inflict severe injury on rivals. The female has much smaller tusks and only pedicels in place of antlers. Muntjac are indigenous to south-eastern China and Taiwan, but have been introduced to England and France and they inhabit dense vegetation and parkland where they feed on grass, shoots and low-growing foliage. They are solitary and elusive and are mainly active at night. The male sheds his antlers in early summer, but regrows them in time for the autumn mating season. The female gives birth to a single young.

♂♀ Musk Ox *Ovibos moschatus*

Today Musk Oxen inhabit the frozen tundra of Arctic North America and Greenland, but they have been extinct in Eurasia since the end of the last Ice Age. They were reintroduced to Spitsbergen in 1929, southern Norway in 1932 and have since spread into parts of neighbouring Sweden. They were also reintroduced to Siberia in 1975. The small summer groups of females (cows) and their young (calves) led by an old male (bull) form larger winter herds of up to 100 animals and feed on grass, lichen, sedge and dwarf Arctic shrubs. Both sexes have horns that grow to 60cm (23.6in). The males are larger than the females and grow to 2.3m (7.5ft) long. Musk Oxen have dense, waterproof, shaggy coats that hang almost to the ground and protect them against the intense cold, while their broad hooves are adapted for travelling over soft snow. In May a single young is born that is initially vulnerable to wolves. When threatened

the herd characteristically forms a circle with the young at the centre and a formidable ring of horns facing out towards their attackers. Musk Oxen are so-named for the musky odour emitted from the bull's facial glands in the summer mating season.

♂♀ Narwhal *Monodon monoceros*

The Narwhal is a whale that lives in the Arctic Ocean where it feeds on squid and crustaceans and can grow as large as 6m (nearly 20ft), excluding its tusk. Adult male Narwhals can weigh up to 1800kg (3969lb), but the females are smaller. The young are born with a mottled grey skin, which gradually pales until it becomes almost pure white in old age. The most conspicuous feature of the mature male Narwhal is the single spiral tusk – actually a modified upper left incisor tooth – which grows as long as 3m (nearly 10ft) and which it is thought is used for fighting and in sexual display. In medieval times unscrupulous traders sold these tusks as the horns of the unicorn. Even today representations of the unicorn often show it sporting the unique spiral Narwhal tusk on its forehead.

♂♀ Nilgai *Boselaphus tragocamelus*

The Nilgai is a large antelope that lives in the forests, low jungle and open plains of the Indian subcontinent where it is preyed on by tigers and leopards. It browses on a wide range of plant matter and also raids fruit and sugar cane plantations. The hornless females (cows) and their young (calves) live in small herds of 6–20 while the horned males (bulls) are solitary or form small bachelor herds. In the mating season the males fight each other on their knees to win females. Twin calves (usually) are born and females are capable of mating again immediately after giving birth. The males acquire their distinctive bluish-grey coats at maturity at about 3 years and are also known as 'Bluebucks'. Nilgai grow to 2–2.1m (6.6–6.9ft) long.

♂♀ Nine-banded Armadillo *Dasypus novemcinctus*

The solitary and nocturnal Nine-banded Armadillo is the most common member of the Armadillo family (Dasypodidae) and can be found in the New World from Texas to northern Argentina. Its protective, horny carapace is articulated to form 8–11, but normally 9, bands, that are connected by soft, flexible skin. When attacked, it withdraws its feet and lowers its tank-like body to the ground for protection. The natural habitat of this creature is bushland where with its powerful forepaws it digs a 1m (3.3ft) deep burrow. This has corridors sometimes as long as 5m (16.4ft) that lead to as many as 12 exits, which constitute escape routes. A peculiarity of the reproductive cycle of the Armadillo is that the egg is only implanted in the uterus several months after fertilization. Usually four identical babies are born, all from the same egg, which has subsequently divided. The Armadillo uses its long, tapering snout to explore excavations made with its paws in anthills and termitaria in

Start among the smallest creatures if you wish to find more couples.
You will have encountered some of them before in this book –
whether you noticed them or not. There's also the previous occupant
of an enormous egg, a well-bred dog, a lonely lover,
a primary pisciform, a pulchritudinous Londoner and the queen
of the jungle. A stagestruck snail is waiting near the wings.

search of food. Its diet also includes spiders, small reptiles and eggs. Size varies but adults typically attain a length of 50cm (19.7in) with a tail of 40cm (15.7in).

♂♀ Norway Lemming *Lemmus lemmus*

Norway Lemmings are to be found in Scandinavia and the Kola Peninsula of Russia where they inhabit the Arctic tundra and grasslands feeding on moss, grass, sedge and dwarf shrubs. They are rodents and are 10–13cm (3.9–5in) long with short 2cm (0.8in) tails. They are active both at day and night and in winter they make extensive runways on the ground beneath the snow so they can continue to feed. In spring Norway Lemmings begin to breed prolifically and up to 8 litters of 1–13 young each can be produced in a year. Every 3–4 years there is a population explosion. In such a 'lemming year', the cause of which is not fully understood, the excess population migrates in vast numbers. Many are eaten en route by predators such as wolves, wolverines, snowy owls and skuas and many more perish as they try to cross rivers or when they eventually come to the sea. Norway Lemmings do not, as popularly believed, deliberately commit suicide.

♂♀ Numbat or Banded Anteater
Myrmecobius fasciatus

The Numbat fills the same ecological niche in its native south-western Australia as the anteater in other parts of the world. This marsupial has strongly clawed forefeet for digging and a long, extensible, sticky tongue capable of being thrust out 15cm (5.9in) to lap up its diet of termites and ants. It has an enormous appetite for these and consumes up to 20,000 each day. The Numbat spends its days alone foraging in the eucalyptus forests, but its numbers have declined drastically since Australia was first settled due to loss of habitat, bush fires and to introduced predators such as dogs, cats and foxes. It is the sole member of the family Myrmecobiidae and between January–May a litter of 2–4 young is produced. These cling to their mother's nipples beneath her fur, as the Numbat does not possess a pouch. Numbats are 21–27.5cm (8.3–10.8in) long with tails of 16–21cm (6.3–8.3in).

♂♀ Nyala *Tragelaphus angasi*

This antelope lives in the dense forests and thickets of south-east Africa. Herds of 8–16, composed of females (cows) and their young (calves) led by an old male (bull), feed on shoots, bark, leaves and fruit of trees that they often stand on their hindlegs to reach. The males have horns up to 83cm (32.7in) long and grow to 150–195cm (59.1–76.8in). The hornless females are much smaller at 135–145cm (53.2–57.1in). Nyalas are preyed on by leopards and lions and the young are also vulnerable to smaller carnivores, eagles and baboons. They are secretive animals active at dawn and dusk. In July–November a single young is born.

♂♀ Ocelot *Felis pardalis*

In the past the Ocelot was widely exploited by the fur trade for its attractive and valuable pelt, the markings of which are as individual as fingerprints. Today this rare cat is a protected species over much of its range from southern Texas, Arizona, Central and South America to northern Argentina. It is a solitary, nocturnal inhabitant of forests, thick bush and marshes where it hunts birds, snakes, agoutis, pacas, peccaries and small mammals. Ocelots are strong swimmers and excellent climbers, and in a den in a hollow tree or in thick vegetation a litter of 2–4 blind young is born. Breeding occurs throughout the year. When fully grown an Ocelot is up to 60–100cm (23.6–39.4in) long with a 30–40cm (11.8–15.8in) tail. The males are larger than the females.

♂♀ Okapi *Okapia johnstoni*

This relative of the giraffe was only discovered in 1900 and is found uniquely in the dense, dark equatorial rainforests of Zaïre where it is believed to live alone or in small groups. Little information about this species in the wild is available due to the inaccessibility of its native habitat, but it has been bred in captivity. The Okapi has a long, prehensile tongue with which it is able to clean its eyes and the male has short, skin-covered horns. The Okapi is similar to the ancestor of the giraffe, as shown by fossil remains. It feeds on loose buds, leaves, shoots, grass, ferns, fruit, fungi, sweet potatoes and manioc. Its principal enemies are the native hunters and the leopard. Female Okapis are larger than the males and their average size is 1.97–2.2m (6.5–7ft) long with tails of 30–42cm (11.8–16.5in).

♂♀ Orang-utan *Pongo pygmaeus*

The Orang-utan is the second largest primate after the gorilla and its name is Malay for 'man of the woods'. Today it is found only on the islands of Borneo and Sumatra where it inhabits the rainforest at altitudes of up to 2000m (6562ft). This gentle, intelligent ape is now rare and in danger of becoming extinct in the wild; there are only an estimated 12,000–20,000 in Borneo and 9000–12,000 in Sumatra. This decline is almost solely due to loss of habitat. Orang-utans are diurnal and arboreal and construct nests 10–20m (32.8–65.6ft) above the ground in which to spend the night. They are generally solitary and they feed on berries, leaves, nuts, insects but mainly on fruit – especially the foul-smelling durian. There is no fixed breeding season and a single young is born that remains with its mother for several years. Adults develop a laryngal sac, which is used to amplify their calls and the males, which are much larger than the females, acquire large flanges of unknown use on either side of the face in old age. Mature Orang-utans are 1.3–1.5m (4–4.9ft) long. Proportionally they have very long arms that, in an old male, can span 2.4m (7.9ft).

♂♀ Plains Viscacha *Lagostomus maximus*

The male Plains Viscacha is much larger than the female and reaches a maximum size of 66cm (26in), with a tail of 20cm (7.9in). It lives on the pampas of Argentina, at altitudes of up to 2680m (8793ft), where it is considered a pest. It excavates extensive burrow systems about 50cm (19.7in) deep, which have as many as 40 entrances, and it eats the grass that is used to raise domestic stock. It is consequently persecuted and is also hunted for its fur and meat. A colony usually consists of 15–30 of these nocturnal rodents but may be much larger and once a year a litter of (usually) 2 young is produced.

♂♀ Platypus *Ornithorhynchus anatinus*

This is a curious creature in many ways, not the least of which is its appearance. When the first specimen was brought to London in the late eighteenth century from Australia, it was widely thought to be a hoax. This semi-aquatic mammal inhabits lakes and rivers where it feeds on crustaceans, aquatic insects and their larvae, frogs and other small animals. It finds these by touching them with its soft, leathery bill as its eyes and ears are situated in folds in its skin, which are closed when underwater. Platypuses are active each night to satisfy their voracious appetites for 1kg (2.2lb) of food a day. The male possesses venomous spurs on its hindfeet, which are used in sexual combat; the poison from these is intensely painful, but not fatal, to man. Platypuses live in short riverbank burrows but in the August–November breeding season the female digs a nesting burrow up to 18m (59ft) long. Platypuses are one of the very few mammals to lay eggs and the female lays 2–3 soft-shelled, sticky eggs. The newly hatched young are just 12.5mm (0.5in) long and are blind and helpless. They lap milk that the nippleless mother excretes on to her fur from slits in the abdominal wall. Their initial teeth are gradually replaced by horny ridges suitable for crushing prey. Platypuses are typically 46cm (18.1in) long with flat, beaver-like tails of 18cm (7in).

♂♀ Polar Bear *Thalarctos maritimus*

Polar Bears are circumpolar in their distribution and they hunt the Arctic ice floes mainly for seals as well as caribou, musk oxen, Arctic hares, fish, seabirds and carrion. In summer they supplement this diet with berries, grass and leaves. They are strong but slow swimmers and can outrun caribou over short distances. They have a thick layer of insulating fat beneath their distinctive waterproof white coats and the soles of their broad feet are furred to facilitate walking across the ice. They have no natural enemies apart from man and their skins have long been valued as trophies. The Innuits make use of their hides, fat, tendons and flesh, though their liver is inedible as it has a high vitamin A content and is poisonous. The male is larger than the female and measures 2.2–2.5m (7.2–8.2ft) overall with a short 7–12cm (2.8–4.7in) tail. Polar Bears mate every second year in April–May and, in January–February, a litter of 1–4 cubs is born in a den beneath the snow.

Porcupine *Hystrix cristata*

The name Porcupine is probably a corruption from the French *Porc-épic* meaning 'spiked pig', which is only half correct as this creature is a rodent. The 'spikes' refer to the long quills that are used in self-defence. When threatened it erects these loosely attached quills and reverses rapidly on to its aggressor, impaling it after first giving a warning by rattling its spiny tail. It cannot shoot these quills as some believe. This species is nocturnal and terrestrial and is distributed in North, West and Central Africa and in southern Italy and Sicily where it was probably introduced by the Romans. It was once an inhabitant of Egypt and appears in carvings of the Fifth and Sixth Dynasties, but it is believed to be extinct there today. Porcupines feed on a wide variety of plant matter and are a pest to root crops and orchards. They live in small groups in burrows and in the summer 1–4 young are born that when adult are 50–70cm (19.7–27.6in) long, with 5–12cm (nearly 2–4.7in) tails.

Pretty-faced Wallaby or Whip-tailed Wallaby *Wallabia elegans*

Wallabies are medium-sized members of the kangaroo family (Macropodidae) and are in many ways identical, apart from their size and some details of dentition. Pretty-faced Wallabies – so called because of their attractive cheek markings – can be found in open woodlands along the coast of north-east Australia. An average male member of this species might measure 92cm (36.2in) with a tail as long as 94cm (37in). The male is larger and heavier than the female. As with its larger kangaroo cousins, a baby is born as a semi-embryo and its development continues in its mother's pouch where it suckles until it becomes independent. Another curious feature of the sexual cycle of this creature is that if for some reason, such as drought, the mother can no longer provide the infant with milk it is expelled from the pouch to die. When food becomes available once more, a reserve embryo, which was produced at the time of the same mating, is implanted in the uterus and a second pregnancy occurs.

Pronghorn *Antilocapra americana*

By the 1920s the Pronghorn had become seriously endangered due to overhunting and its numbers reduced from its one-time estimated population of more than 35 million to less than 20,000. Since then it has been protected and its numbers are now sufficient to allow controlled hunting once more in parts of its range. It is distributed from Central Canada through western USA to Mexico where it inhabits the open prairies and deserts at altitudes of up to 3350m (10,991ft) and feeds on grass, weeds and shrubs. Both sexes have two-pronged horns, though those of the male are much longer at about 25cm (nearly 10in). It is a good swimmer and a superbly swift runner able to achieve speeds of 70km/h (44mph) for up to 2km (1.2 miles). It can leap 6m (19.7ft) in a single bound and lope along at speeds of 50km/h (31mph) for 30 minutes or more. It normally lives in groups of up to 8 led by a male but in autumn it forms herds of up to 1000. In the breeding season the males battle to collect a 'harem' and in spring 1–3 young are born that when only 4 days old are capable of running faster than a man. It is the only representative of the family Antilocapridae and grows to 1–1.5m (3.3–4.9ft) with a 7.5–18cm (almost 3–7in) tail.

Przewalski's Horse or Wild Horse *Equus ferus*

In 1881 the Russian explorer Nikolay Przewalsky returned from a journey in western Mongolia with news of a dun-coloured, primitive wild horse. He reported it was about 12–14 hands (1.3–1.4m or 4.1–4.7ft) with low withers, a narrow back, a short, steep croup, an erect mane and sparse tail. This horse is the closest relative to modern domestic horses and ponies and probably carried the Mongol warriors on their great conquests. In Paleolithic times (about 2.5 million years ago) Wild Horses were present over much of Eurasia, but they probably became extinct in western Europe in the early Holocene period (about 9000 years ago). In 1901 an expedition brought back a small number of females (mares) and males (stallions) that formed the basis of the present day zoo stock. Przewalski's Horse is very hardy and can survive the intense cold and feed on the poorest of pasture. It is able to sprint over short distances at speeds of up to 70km/h (43.5mph), and to maintain 50km/h (31mph) over longer ones. This horse would have provided the nomadic peoples not only with a means of transport but also with meat, milk, hides and fuel in the form of dung.

Raccoon *Procyon lotor*

These animals are nocturnal and are easily recognizable by their ringed tails and mask-like facial markings, which give them a roguish, bandit-like appearance. Raccoons are omnivorous, intelligent and highly adaptable creatures and are often found scavenging in suburban regions where they can become a nuisance by raiding dustbins, though their preferred foods are melons, corn, birds' eggs and nestlings. They are found from southern Canada, through the United States as far south as Panama. They like to live near water and have the curious habit of using their dexterous forepaws to wash their food – even frogs and fish. They are agile climbers and make their dens in hollow trees where they sleep, rather than truly hibernate, for prolonged periods during very cold weather. Although they can be savage fighters when cornered, Raccoons are reportedly easily trained and make charming pets. Unfortunately, in recent years, Raccoons have been one of the species responsible for the gradual spread of rabies, which has now become a threat to domestic mammals, and therefore to humans. A fully grown Raccoon measures 75–90cm (29.5–35.4in), including its tail of 25cm (nearly 10in).

Raccoon-dog *Nyctereutes procyonoides*

The facial similarity of the Raccoon-dog to the Raccoon *Procyon lotor* earns it its common name but the resemblance ends there. This member of the dog family (Canidae) is indigenous to eastern China and Japan but was introduced to Russia in the 1930s for its commercially valuable fur, known as 'Ussurian Raccoon', and from there it has spread into Central Europe. Raccoon-dogs are primarily nocturnal and they live alone in rock dens, hollow trees or abandoned burrows in forested areas never far from water. They are more omnivorous than foxes and rodents, birds, amphibians, reptiles, fish, acorns, fruit, berries, bulbs, earthworms, carrion and scavenged human refuse all form part of their diet. Unlike foxes they undergo a period of winter inactivity emerging from time to time on mild nights. Raccoon-dogs mate once a year and 6–8 young are born. They grow to an adult size of 50–55cm (19.7–21.7in) with 13–18cm (5.1–7in) tails.

Ratel or Honey-badger *Mellivora capensis*

A small African bird, the Greater or Black-throated Honeyguide *Indicator indicator*, is inordinately fond of honey, beeswax and bee larvae but is incapable of breaking into nests to obtain them. Not so the powerfully built Ratel and the two have developed a symbiotic relationship whereby the honeyguide attracts the Ratel's attention by rattling its tail feathers and, flying ahead a short distance at a time, leads it to the nest. The Ratel is protected by its tough hide and, after it has torn the nest apart with its strong foreclaws and eaten its fill, the honeyguide feasts on the leftovers. The Ratel's diet is supplemented with insects, fruit, birds' eggs and occasionally animals larger than itself up to the size of sheep or small antelopes. The nocturnal Ratel is found on the savannas and in forested regions of sub-Saharan Africa, the Middle East and northern India and lives alone or in pairs in 1–3m (3.3–9.8ft) long burrows. It is a ferocious fighter and if attacked it can inflict savage wounds with its jaws. A litter of 1–2 young is born and when fully grown the Ratel measures 83–100cm (32.7–39.4in) long; males are larger than females.

Red Deer *Cervus elaphus*

The Red Deer of temperate Eurasia and north-west Africa is conspecific with the Wapiti *C. canadensis* of North America (also known there as the Elk). It has been introduced into New Zealand. The males (stags or harts) are larger than the females (hinds) and grow to a maximum size of 2.5m (8.2ft) long. The males bear antlers that are shed in spring and regrown by autumn and have, on a mature animal, up to 14 points (tines). Red Deer usually remain hidden during the day and emerge at dusk to feed on grass, shoots, leaves, shrubs, beechmast and acorns and they occasionally raid crops. They live primarily in woodland in matriarchal herds; the males, which live separately for most of the year, fight with each other in the autumn 'rut' to win a harem of females. A single, speckled young is produced that is suckled for 3–4 months and becomes independent after 1 year.

Most of these animals you have encountered before,
but there's also a Zimbabwean couple, a Scandinavian one too,
a sinful mustelid, a tantalizing fiddler, a cunning canine,
an antipodean trio and a musical mollusc (but it doesn't count).

♂♀ **Red Fox** *Vulpes vulpes*

Long a byword for craftiness, the natural cunning of this member of the dog family (Canidae) has contributed greatly to its success in the human environment. Highly adaptable, the Red Fox is found in a wide range of habitats, including open country, woodland and, increasingly in recent years, in urban environments where it lives off rats, mice and human refuse. In the wild its diet includes rabbits, rodents, birds – sometimes including domestic poultry – insects, earthworms, carrion, fruit and berries. There are many tales of foxes 'charming' prey: for instance, they will appear to be intent solely on playing and when a curious animal comes too close to investigate this odd behaviour it is seized and eaten. Red Foxes are principally nocturnal and solitary, coming together only to breed. In spring a litter of (usually) 4 young (cubs) is born to the female (vixen) in a short burrow (earth). The cubs and the mother are brought food by the male (dog) until they are old enough to follow her on nightly foraging trips. Red Foxes are distributed over most of temperate Eurasia to Japan, North Africa, and the majority of North America. They have also been introduced into Australia and measure 46–86cm (18.1–33.9in) with a broad, white-tipped tail (brush) of 30.5–55.5cm (12–21.9in). They are widely persecuted by farmers for the depredations they reputedly make among domestic fowl and in Britain they are hunted on horseback for sport.

♂♀ **Red Howler Monkey** *Alouatta seniculus*

Red Howler Monkeys are named after the male's extremely loud territorial call, which is made most often in the mornings and can carry for 3–5km (1.9–3.1miles). Red Howler Monkeys are almost exclusively arboreal and live in the rainforests of South America where they feed on leaves and fruit. They are diurnal and travel in small groups of 6–8 led by an old male. Among the largest of the New World monkeys, the sturdily built Red Howler Monkey grows to 80–90cm (31.5–35.5in) and has a prehensile tail. This has a tip that is naked on the underside to facilitate grip. Males are larger than females and their main enemies are eagles and the larger carnivores. Mating occurs throughout the year and a single young is born that is dependent on its mother for several years, initially clinging to her underfur and later riding on her back.

♂♀ **Red Kangaroo** *Macropus rufus*

The name Kangaroo is in itself an oddity. When early European explorers in Australia asked their Aboriginal guides the name of the creatures they saw bounding across their native semi-arid grassland, they pointed and exclaimed 'Kangaroo!' which, in the Aboriginal tongue, means 'there he goes!'. Even if the story is apocryphal, the name stuck and is applied to the larger species of this marsupial – the smaller are known as Rat Kangaroos and the medium-sized ones as Wallabies. The Red Kangaroo is one of the biggest with large males (boomers) measuring 1.5–1.8m (4.9–5.9ft) with a tail of up to 1m (3.3ft). After mating the smaller

female – which despite the 'visual pun' in the picture actually has a bluish-grey coat – gives birth to a single young (joey). It emerges only partly developed and measures 2cm (0.8in), and at 0.75g (0.03oz) is just 1/30,000th of its mother's weight. It climbs unassisted into her pouch where it suckles for about a further 240 days. Red Kangaroos have several predators including man, who still hunts this beast for its meat and fine hide despite strict controls. A group of Kangaroos is known as a mob.

♂♀ **Reindeer or Caribou** *Rangifer tarandus*

Known as the Caribou in North America, the Reindeer is the only deer whose female bears antlers. It inhabits the Arctic tundra of northern Eurasia and North America where it feeds on grass and other plants but in the winter it sustains itself on Reindeer Moss *Cladonia rangiferina*, an abundant spongy, fruticose lichen that it uncovers from beneath the snow. Its range and numbers have been much reduced due to overhunting and some local populations have been wiped out. Reindeer are extremely hardy and can survive very low temperatures. They have broad hooves that allow them to travel over soft snow. They undertake long seasonal migrations. In northern Scandinavia and Russia they have been domesticated and provide meat, hides and milk as well as being seemingly tireless pack animals. Domestic Reindeer are smaller than wild deer and measure 1.2–2.2m (3.9–7.2ft) overall with tails of 7–21cm (2.8–8.3in). Males live apart from the large matriarchal herds, only coming together for the September–October rut when they battle to gather together a harem of 5–40 females to mate with. A single young is born that can run with the herd within just a few hours.

♂♀ **Ring-tailed Lemur** *Lemur catta*

The Ring-tailed Lemur is the most common of the approximately 16 species of lemur, which are confined to Madagascar and the Comoro Islands. They live in troops of up to 20 dominated by females, within well-defined territories. The boundaries of these are marked with secretions from scent glands on the forelimbs, chin and genital areas. Ring-tailed Lemurs are diurnal. They are expert climbers and feed on grass, fruit, leaves, flowers, bark and resin. They typically measure 45cm (17.7in) with 55cm (21.7in) tails and their main enemies are fossas and raptors. They mate in April–June and (usually) a single young is born, but twins or triplets occur in 15 per cent of births. The young initially cling to their mother's belly but later ride on her back.

♂♀ **Rufous Rat-kangaroo**
Aepyprymnus rufescens

Rufous Rat-kangaroos are among the smallest members of the Kangaroo family and are generally no bigger than large rabbits, growing to a maximum of 52cm (20.4in) with tails of 40cm (15.7in). They are nocturnal and forage in the undergrowth of their native eastern Australia for worms, grubs, fungi and plant

matter. Although little is known of their breeding habits, they reproduce slowly, producing no more than 2 young each year.

♂♀ **Sable Antelope** *Hippotragus niger*

Sable, the heraldic term for black, refers to the colour of the upper half of the adult male antelope. The females and immature antelopes are a dark reddish-brown. Both sexes have horns but those of the male are much larger, growing up to 1.6m (5.2ft). These have been much sought after as trophies, which have contributed to the decline of this species. Sable Antelopes are found in small troops in the open woods and thick bushveld of East and south-east Africa where they feed on grass and foliage. Males are larger than females and an adult measures nearly 2–2.1m (6.5–6.9ft) long with a tail of 38–46cm (about 15–18.1in). A single young is born at any season.

♂♀ **Saiga** *Saiga tatarica*

The most curious feature of the Saiga is its enlarged nose, which has downward-pointing nostrils that are lined with hairs, mucous tracts and glands. Saigas have a keen sense of smell, but it is believed the principal function of their nose is to warm and moisturize the frigid air of their native habitat as they inhale. Today they inhabit the bleak, windswept steppes of Kazakhstan, Turkestan, southern Siberia, and parts of Mongolia and China, but in former times they also ranged over much of eastern Europe. They were hunted to just c.1000 animals by 1920 but, since becoming a protected species in 1923, their numbers have increased to more than 2 million and controlled hunting is allowed once more. Each autumn Saigas form vast migratory herds and move south feeding on grass and low-growing shrubs – including those poisonous to other species. They return north in spring when males battle to collect a harem of females. Between 1–3 young are born that eventually grow to measure 1–1.4m (3.3–4.6ft) with short tails of 6–12cm (2.4–4.7in). The 30–35cm (11.8–13.8in) horns, which are only worn by the larger and more robust males, were an important ingredient of traditional Chinese medicine. Saigas can run for long distances at 60km/h (37.3mph) and sprint at speeds of up to 80km/h (49.7mph).

♂♀ **Serval** *Felis serval*

The long legs of this cat enable it to leap up and grab low-flying birds from the air but it also preys, in a less spectacular fashion, on mammals up to the size of small antelopes, ground-living birds, lizards, fish and insects. Grass and fruit are also eaten. Servals are widely persecuted for their killing of domestic poultry and they are hunted for their fur. Gifted with keen senses of sight and hearing, Servals are diurnal and solitary and inhabit the plains, savannas and woodlands of sub-Saharan Africa at altitudes of up to 3000m (9843ft). Mating takes place throughout the year and 1–4 young are born, often in the abandoned burrow of another species. Servals are 67–100cm (26.4–39.4in) long with tails of 24–45cm (9.5–17.7in).

Siamang *Hylobates syndactylus*

The Siamang is the largest of the gibbons and grows to a length of 75–90cm (29.6–35.5in). It inhabits the mountain rainforests of Malaysia and Sumatra at altitudes of up to 1800m (5905ft) where it lives in family groups of parents and 1 or 2 offspring. It feeds on fruit, leaves, shoots, flowers, insects and, occasionally, birds' eggs. It is mainly distinguishable from the other gibbons by its large size and by its dilatable naked throat sac, which is used to amplify its territorial calls that are audible for up to 4km (2.5 miles). Its range is now much reduced due to loss of habitat through logging and its current numbers probably do not exceed 100,000. The Siamang is extremely agile and arboreal, rarely descending to the ground; it passes the nights on high branches. A single, hairless young is born that initially clings to its mother.

Slender Loris *Loris tardigradus*

During the day the Slender Loris sleeps in the treetops rolled into a ball, but as night falls it awakes and begins its ponderous locomotion among the branches. It forages for insects, lizards, tree frogs, small birds and their eggs, shoots and leaves. It lives in the dense forests of southern India and Sri Lanka from low-lying swamps to altitudes of up to 1800m (5905ft) in the mountains. The Slender Loris is normally solitary, coming together only to breed twice a year and in May and December (usually) a single young is produced. It is tailless and reaches a size of 17.5–26.4cm (6.9–10.4in).

Snowshoe Hare or Varying Hare *Lepus americanus*

Snowshoe or Varying Hares earn their common names respectively from their large, thickly haired feet, which both insulate and distribute their weight allowing them easy passage across soft snow, and for the seasonal variation of their coat, which changes from brownish in summer to a camouflage of pure white in winter. They are distributed in North America from Alaska through Canada to the United States and their diet is succulent plants and grass in summer and twigs, bark, shoots and buds in winter. Their main enemies are the lynx and fox. Between 2–3 litters are produced a year starting in March. The 1–7 young are born in a concealed nest protected from the elements. They are born furred and open-eyed and grow to 36–52cm (14.2–20.5in) with 2.5–5.5cm (nearly 1–2.2in) tails.

Southern Sea-lion or South American Sea-lion *Otaria flavescens*

Sea-lions have external ears and the ability to rotate their hind flippers forward so that they can move more easily on land than seals. At 2.5m (8.2ft) long and weighing up to 520kg (1146lb), the maned male Southern Sea-lions are very much larger than the females, which rarely weigh more than 150kg (about 330lb). Their breeding grounds are from the Isla Lobos de Tierra off

Peru south to Cape Horn and the Falkland Islands. The males compete for the best territories and establish a harem of 3–20 females with which to mate. The resulting embryo lies dormant and is only implanted when birth of the single offspring is ensured for the optimum time the following year. They feed on fish and cephalopods and are unpopular with commercial fishermen, who often kill them for the damage they cause to nets.

Sperm Whale *Physeter catodon*

The Sperm Whale is the largest of the Odontoceti, or toothed whales, that grows to a maximum length of 20m (over 65ft) and weighs as much as 35,000–50,000kg (77,175–110,250lb), though females are generally only half this size. Sperm Whales are reported to have dived to the astonishing depth of 2500m (over 8202ft) or nearly six times as deep as the Empire State Building is high in search of their main diet of giant deepwater cephalopods, which they locate by a form of sonar. Near the nasal passages in the front of their huge heads is a mass of a waxy substance known as spermaceti. Sperm Whales have the largest brain of any mammal; they weigh 9.2kg (20.3lb). Until fairly recently Sperm Whales were extensively hunted for their oil, meat and ambergris. This last substance – a solid intestinal secretion that develops a pleasant odour when exposed to sunlight – is widely used to fix the scent of expensive perfumes and as a cooking spice in the Orient.

Spotted Hyaena or Laughing Hyaena *Crocuta crocuta*

The Spotted Hyaena is found in most dry, open places in sub-Saharan Africa at altitudes of up to 4500m (14,764ft) where it lives in clans of up to 80. Within a clan the larger females outrank the males and the clan's territory is vigorously guarded and defended. The Spotted Hyaena is a largely nocturnal scavenger and feeds mainly on carrion, often following lions to feed on their leftovers. It devours skin, hair and even bones, which it crushes with its immensely powerful jaws. A clan of these formidable creatures is capable of driving a lion, cheetah or leopard from its kill. The Spotted Hyaena's blood-curdling 'laugh' is cried after a successful kill when it rapidly gorges itself on up to 15kg (33lb) at one time. The Spotted Hyaena is the largest species of hyaena and measures 95–165cm (37.4–65in) with a tail of 25–36cm (9.9–14.2in). A litter of 1–2 young can be produced at any time of the year.

Springbuck or Springbok *Antidorcus marsupialis*

Before the arrival of the settlers, herds of a million or more Springbucks made migratory journeys of several days' duration across the savannas and veld of their native southern Africa. But they were mercilessly hunted and today these herds rarely number more than 1500. They acquired their name from their habit of leaping up to 3.5m (11.5ft) into the air when they become excited, which is known as 'pronking'. Also in times of

excitement, they open a long, glandular pouch along their back and erect a crest of stiff, white hair. They are capable of running at speeds of up to 90km/h (55.9mph) with bounds of as much as 15m (49.2ft). Both sexes possess horns, which are up to 48cm (18.9in) long in the male, and they are 120–140cm (47.3–55.2in) in length. Springbucks are diurnal and feed on grass and the foliage of bushes that they stand on their hindlegs to reach. They reproduce throughout the year and 1 (rarely 2) young are born. Their main predators are the large cats.

Spring Hare *Pedetes capensis*

The Spring Hare is not a hare at all but a rodent and is indigenous to southern and East Africa where it inhabits open, sandy country and feeds on bulbs, grain, roots and other vegetable matter, and possibly on insects. It is nocturnal and lives in burrows several metres (or yards) long. It normally hops along on all fours but in flight it hops on its long hindlegs, like a kangaroo, making leaps of up to 8m (26.2ft), and using its long tail as a counterbalance. It has many enemies, including large and small carnivores, snakes and birds of prey. Between 1–2 young are produced. Fully grown Spring Hares measure 35–43cm (13.8–16.9in) with tails of a similar length.

Squirrel Monkey *Saimiri sciureus*

Omnivorous Squirrel Monkeys live in bands of up to 30 that sometimes join other bands to form large troops of some 100 in the forests and cultivated land of South America from Colombia to the Amazon basin where they are the most common primate. At night they sleep in the trees huddled together and in the day they process in single file after the band leader along well-worn arboreal pathways to forage for nuts, fruit, insects, spiders, lizards and small birds and their eggs. A single young is born, which initially clings to the back of its mother, but soon becomes independent. An adult Squirrel Monkey is 26–36cm (10.2–14.2in) long with a non-prehensile tail of 35–42cm (13.8–16.5in).

Stoat or Ermine *Mustela erminea*

In the north of its range, the winter coat of the Stoat is pure white except for the black tip of its tail; the fur, and the creature in winter, is known as Ermine. It is one of the finest and most valuable of furs once used exclusively in Europe for the robes of royalty and high-ranking nobility. Stoats have voracious appetites and prey on rodents, fish, frogs, birds and their eggs and insects. They even kill prey much larger than themselves, such as rabbits and hares. Ruthless and efficient killers, their prey is despatched by a swift and powerful bite on the back of the neck. Stoats are inhabitants of the forests and tundra and are distributed over the temperate and Arctic parts of Eurasia, North America and Greenland. They have been introduced into New Zealand. The males are considerably larger than the females and grow to a maximum size of 29cm (11.4in) with tails of 9cm (3.5in), but in the south they may grow bigger. Mating takes

Try to find the earthy tenant of the second house,

a crowned clarinettist, a diminutive drummer and a jumping J.

This is the ultimate detail in this book and the end of the hunt.

By now you have looked at all 707 animals. You looked at

353 of them twice and one only once.

But did you *see* it?

place in the summer but due to the delayed implantation of the embryo the litter of 4–12 blind young (usually about 6) is not produced until the following spring.

♂♀ Streaked Tenrec or Banded Tenrec
Hemicentetes semispinosus

The Streaked Tenrec is found on Madagascar only and is an inhabitant of the forest edge and scrub. It is chiefly nocturnal and forages on the forest floor, using its flexible snout to root up grubs and earthworms. It rolls itself into a ball and uses the prickly spines on its back as a defence when threatened. Tenrecs retain some primitive characteristics such as a cloaca. They are one of the most fecund of the insectivores, producing a litter of up to 11 young between December–March. Streaked Tenrecs are 16–19cm (6.3–7.5in) long with vestigial tails only. They do not hibernate but periods of cool weather are spent in inactivity.

♂♀ Striped Skunk or Common Skunk
Mephitis mephitis

The conspicuous black and white markings of the Striped Skunk are a warning display to would-be predators. If an aggressor is foolish enough to persist, it is repelled by a spray of a yellowish and intensely unpleasant liquid from the skunk's anal gland. This spray is so foul-smelling that it can momentarily stop the aggressor's breathing and cause temporary blindness if it hits the eyes. Surprisingly, this secretion, which can be ejected with considerable accuracy for distances up to 3.7m (12.1ft) and be smelt for almost 1km (0.6 mile), provides a base for some perfumes. Striped Skunks are distributed in most regions of North America from southern Canada to northern Mexico. They live in self-dug or abandoned burrows or beneath buildings. They are nocturnal and omnivorous and feed on mice, birds and their eggs, insects, berries and carrion. They also raid domestic poultry runs. The males engage in ritual combat before mating and a litter of 5–6 blind, naked young (kits) is born in spring. Striped Skunks are 31–46cm (12.2–18.1in) long with bushy tails of 18–40cm (7–15.8in).

♂♀ Sumatran Rhinoceros
Dicerorhinus sumatrensis

This is the smallest species of rhinoceros. It achieves a body length of 2.4–3.2m (7.8–10.5ft), a tail of about 60cm (23.6in) and a weight of 1–2 tonnes (2205–4410lb). Until the present century this beast was distributed over most of south-east Asia, but it has been hunted almost to extinction for its so-called 'medicinal' value in traditional Asian remedies so that today no more than 850 are extant in isolated populations. Those that remain inhabit the dense forests of Sumatra, Borneo, Burma, Thailand and Malaysia where they feed on fruit, leaves, twigs and bamboo shoots. Rhinos have 2 horns and are covered with bristly hairs. They are normally solitary, only pairing in the

breeding season. A single young is produced that stays with its mother for about 2 years.

♂♀ Takin *Budorcas taxicolor*

The Takin is a shy animal that inhabits dense rhododendron and bamboo thickets in Bhutan, Burma and the Chinese provinces of Shensi and Szechwan at altitudes of between 2400–4250m (7874–13,944ft). Both sexes have 60cm (23.6in) long horns and they live in herds, though the older males are solitary. The Takin's diet is grass and alpine herbage and in winter it descends to lower altitudes and splits up into smaller groups, grazing on grass, bamboo and tree shoots. A single young is born in March–April. When fully grown a Takin is about 1.2m (3.9ft) long with a 10cm (3.9in) tail. The Takin is hunted for its meat.

♂♀ Talapoin *Miopithecus talapoin*

The Talapoin is the smallest of the true monkeys of Africa and grows to 25–40cm (nearly 10–15.8in) with a tail of 36–52cm (14.2–20.5in). It can swim and dive well and is always found near water in the mangroves and tropical rainforests of Central Africa. It lives in troops of 12–20 that sometimes join with others to form larger groups of up to 80. Each troop travels along well-used arboreal trails to forage each day for fruit, seeds, leaves, insects, birds' eggs and small vertebrates. The Talapoin also frequently raids plantations and in some areas it is considered a pest. Talapoins mate in May–September. A single young is produced. Talapoins are preyed on by leopards, genets, snakes and raptors.

♂♀ Tamandua or Lesser Anteater
Tamandua tetradactyla

Unlike its much larger relative, the terrestrial Giant Anteater *Myrmecophaga tridactyla*, the Tamandua is arboreal and rarely descends to the ground. It spends its life searching the treetops of the tropical rainforests of southern Mexico, Central and South America to Brazil and Bolivia for termites and ants. It breaks open their nests with its powerful foreclaws and catches its prey with its long, protrusible, sticky tongue. It is a nocturnal creature and grows to 54–58cm (21.3–22.9in) with a prehensile tail of 54.5–55.5cm (21.5–21.9in), which is naked on the underside to facilitate its grip on branches. Tamanduas are usually solitary and come together only briefly in the mating season. Little accurate breeding information is available, but a single young is born that is initially carried on its mother's back.

♂♀ Tantalus Monkey *Cercopithecus aethiops*

In the myths of ancient Greece Tantalus was the son of Zeus and Pluto who stole ambrosia – the food of the gods – and gave it to men. For this he was punished in Hades by standing neck-deep in water that receded when he tried to drink it and under fruit he could never reach. From his ordeal we get the word 'tantalize', though it is unclear just why his name is applied to

this monkey, which is indigenous to sub-Saharan Africa from the River Volta to Ethiopia. The Tantalus Monkey is diurnal and inhabits the savannas and steppes, in groups of 6–60, where it forages for fruit, berries, seeds, bark, shoots, insects, lizards, birds and their eggs, and sometimes raids cultivated crops. Mainly ground-living during the day, it sleeps in trees and is 40–83cm (15.8–32.7in) long with a tail of 50–114cm (19.7–44.9in). The males are larger than the females and they breed throughout the year. A single young is produced.

♂♀ Three-toed Sloth *Bradypus tridactylus*

This proverbially sluggish animal spends almost its entire life upside down suspended from branches by its hook-shaped claws. Its fur even grows downwards to shed the plentiful rain that occurs in the tropical forests of Central and South America where it lives. A single-celled green algae grows on this fur which, together with its ponderously slow movements, probably contributes to the camouflage of this otherwise defenceless creature. The Three-toed Sloth has 8 or 9 neck vertebrae instead of other mammals' usual 7 and these give its head extra mobility, allowing it to be turned round through an arc of 270 degrees. It has a 4-chambered stomach, which contains bacteria and protozoans that aid in the digestion of the mainstay of its diet – the tough leaves of the Trumpet Tree *Cecropia peltata*. It is solitary and nocturnal with poorly developed senses of sight and smell. Three-toed Sloths breed throughout the year and a single young is born. This animal is preyed on by jaguars and ocelots and is especially vulnerable when it descends to the ground every 7–10 days to defecate. It is 50–60cm (19.7–23.6in) long with a short 6.5–7cm (2.6–2.8in) tail.

♂♀ Tiger *Panthera tigris*

The Tiger is the largest and most powerfully built member of the cat family (Felidae). A large male specimen measures 2.8m (over 9ft) with a tail of 1m (3.3ft) and weighs as much as 290kg (nearly 640lb). The largest Tigers are still found in Siberia, where they originated, but they become progressively smaller and more brightly coloured further south in their range, such as those in Java and Sumatra. The distinctive stripes of the Tiger provide it with superb camouflage in the grassland, swamps and light forests that are its native habitat over most of its range. Males and females are of a similar size and their chief difference is the larger cheek whiskers of the male. These shy, solitary, nocturnal carnivores are excellent climbers and can gallop at impressive speeds when chasing their prey such as gaur, deer, wild pigs and buffalo; there are even records of large Tigers attacking elephants. After mating the male leaves the female to give birth alone to 1–6 cubs, which stay with their mother for 2 years.

♂♀ Vicuña *Vicugna vicugna*

The Vicuña is a wild llama that inhabits the semi-arid montane grasslands of western South America from Peru to northern

Chile at altitudes of more than 4000m (13,124ft). It was once more widely distributed and kept throughout the Inca period for its fine wool, but after the arrival of the European settlers it was hunted for its meat and hides. This reduced its numbers from an estimated pre-Columbian total of c.1.5 million to c.10,000 by the 1960s. It has since become a protected species and numbers are slowly increasing. Today there are an estimated 80,000. It lives in small herds of up to 15 led by a male and the surplus males form nomadic bachelor herds. It is smaller than the domesticated llama and is 1.3–1.9m (4.2–6.2ft) long with a short 15–25cm (5.9–9.9in) tail. Even at such high altitudes it is capable of running at speeds of 47km/h (over 29mph) for considerable distances and it feeds mainly on grass and small alpine plants. The female gives birth to a single young, which is suckled for about 10 months.

♂♀ **Virginia Opossum** *Didelphis virginiana*

This is the only marsupial to live in North America and, probably because of the mother's habit of cleaning out her pouch immediately before birth, it was once believed that it gave birth via the nipples in so-called 'mammary gestation' or via the nose. Between 8–18 minute, semi-embryonic young are born, which at 1cm (0.4in) are no larger than honey-bees, and which crawl into the mother's pouch and attach themselves to one of her (usually) 13 nipples. The supernumerary young cannot survive. The ones that do remain in the pouch for 4–5 weeks and emerge to travel about on their mother's back after 8–9 weeks. The adult Virginia Opossum measures 32.5–50cm (12.8–19.7in) with a 25.5–53.5cm (10–21in) naked, prehensile tail and weighs up to 5.5kg (12.1lb). It is a nocturnal and largely arboreal inhabitant of the forests and scrubland of southern Canada, the USA and Central and South America where it feeds on a wide variety of foodstuffs, including rodents, small reptiles, birds, insects and earthworms. It also raids domestic poultry runs and scavenges among human refuse. Virginia Opossums are preyed on by bobcats, coyotes, foxes and raptors and if they are caught they feign death in a behaviour known as 'playing possum'. The predator, which is interested in live prey only, soon loses interest and the Opossum survives.

♂♀ **Walrus or Morse** *Odobenus rosmarus*

Mature male Walruses, which can measure 3.7m (over 12ft) and weigh over 1260kg (2778lb), are much larger than the females that are collected together into 'harems' during the breeding season and presided over by a dominant male. Both sexes have the distinctive tusks – up to 1m (3.3ft) long in the male – which it is believed are used to dig out its principal diet of molluscs from the seabed. Walruses breed every other year; the female bears a single pup that stays with its mother for 2 years. Walruses are to be found in the Arctic and are hunted by the Innuit for their tusks, which are known commercially as 'sea ivory'.

♂♀ **Warthog** *Phacochoerus aethiopicus*

The Warthog is named after the wart-like protuberances on the side of its head, which are more pronounced in the larger male than in the female. The same is true of the tusks. Warthogs live on the savannas of sub-Saharan Africa in family groups and though, like all pigs, they are omnivores, they feed mainly on plant matter. They often shelter from the midday heat or spend the night in deserted aardvark burrows, which they enter backwards so they can defend themselves from predators like lions and leopards. Despite their forbidding appearance, Warthogs are inoffensive and gregarious animals. A male might measure 1.4m (over 4.6ft), excluding his tail, and have curved tusks as long as 60cm (almost 2ft). The tail of up to 50cm (19.7in) is carried erect when it is running.

♂♀ **Waterbuck** *Kobus ellipsiprymnus*

Waterbucks, as one might expect, spend much of their time near water and take refuge in reed beds, submerging themselves up to the nose when threatened. They live in herds of up to 25 led by an old male; other males form bachelor herds. They feed mainly on grass on the savannas and woodlands of sub-Saharan Africa where their main enemies are lions, leopards and hunting dogs, packs of which attack calves and even fully grown females, though they do not prefer their flesh as it has a musky taint. The large 50–99.7cm (19.7–39.2in), crescent-shaped horns are worn only by the males, which are 20–25 per cent larger and heavier than the females and reach a length of 2.2m (7.2ft) with a 45cm (17.7in) tail. A single young (usually) is produced.

♂♀ **Water Buffalo** *Bubalus bubalis*

Although there are at least 75 million domesticated Water Buffalo and a great number of feral animals, their numbers in the wild probably do not exceed 2000. They were originally inhabitants of India and south-east Asia where they have been used as draught animals since before 3000 BC, but they have been subsequently introduced to Japan, the Philippines, Australia, Hawaii, Central and South America, Africa and Europe. Both sexes have horns that, in the male, can grow to 1.2m (3.9ft) measured along the curve. Water Buffalo are 2.4–3m (7.9–9.8ft) long with tails of 0.6–1m (23.6–39.3in) and weigh 0.7–1.2 tonnes (1543–2646lb). These massive beasts have no natural enemies and are avoided even by tigers. True to their common name they live in herds near water where they submerge themselves up to the nose and wallow in the mud, which protects against biting insects. Water Buffalo are herbivorous and feed mainly on lush waterside grass and vegetation. In the breeding season the males, which normally live apart from the rest of the herd, gather a harem with which to mate and 1–2 young are born. One of the best-known by-products of the Water Buffalo is the stringy mozzarella cheese made from its milk, which is the essential ingredient for garnishing a real pizza.

♂♀ **Water Chevrotain** *Hyemoschus aquaticus*

The Water Chevrotain, though larger than the Asiatic Chevrotains, is only the size of a hare. It is 85–100cm (33.5–39.4in) long, including its tail. It is solitary and nocturnal and is always found near water in the forests of West and Central Africa. During the day it remains concealed in dense undergrowth or in a hole in a riverbank, emerging at night to feed on fruit, grass, leaves, insects, crustaceans, fish, worms and small mammals. It is preyed on by leopards, golden cats and civets and escapes by hiding underwater. Following mating, the female gives birth to a single young.

♂♀ **Weasel** *Mustela nivalis*

The Weasel is the smallest carnivore. Its diet chiefly consists of voles and mice and it is agile enough to follow its prey into burrows. The Weasel also takes birds and their eggs as well as animals as large as rabbits. It hunts both by day and by night. Males are noticeably larger than females and the largest that they are likely to grow is 30cm (nearly 12in), including their tail of 7cm (2.8in), though they are commonly smaller. The Weasel is found throughout Europe, North and Central Asia, North Africa and North America and has been introduced into New Zealand. In the extreme northern part of its range, such as Canada, Scandinavia and Russia, it acquires a white coat in winter and tends to be smaller than those in the south. It mates in the spring and produces 2 litters of 4–6 young each year.

♂♀ **Western Tarsier or Horsfield's Tarsier** *Tarsius bancanus*

This small primate is a prodigious leaper both in the trees and on the ground. It can jump a distance of 1.7m (5.6ft) and as high as 60cm (23.6in). The Western Tarsier is 12–15.5cm (4.7–6in) long and has a slender, naked, fur-tipped tail of 18–22.5cm (7–8.9in). Today its numbers are declining due to loss of its native forest habitat on Sumatra and Borneo where it feeds on insects and their larvae, lizards and amphibians, which it pounces on and seizes with its forepaws. The tips of its digits are broadened into adhesive pads that facilitate its mainly arboreal existence. The Western Tarsier is nocturnal. It breeds throughout the year and the female bears a single young, which is active almost at once.

♂♀ **White Rhinoceros or Square-lipped Rhinoceros** *Ceratotherium simum*

Although not truly white, the White Rhinoceros is paler than the other species and is also the largest. It has a body length of up to 5m (16.4ft), a tail of 1m (3.3ft) and a top weight of 3.6 tonnes (7938lb). Nowadays it is found only in isolated populations within protected areas of East and southern Africa and, like all rhinoceroses, it is an endangered species, numbering no more than 5600. This decline in its numbers is mostly due to poaching for its horns, which grow to over 1.5m (4.9ft). In the Orient these have a value equal, almost, to their weight in gold and are believed to have medicinal powers. White Rhinoceroses feed solely on grass on open savanna and in lightly wooded areas and are more gregarious than other rhinos with several animals sharing the same territory. A single young is born at any time of the year. White Rhinoceroses are fond of wallowing in mud and, apart from man, they have no natural enemies.

♂♀ Wild Boar *Sus scrofa*

The Wild Boar – a name applied to both sexes – is the ancestor of the modern domestic pig and is distributed throughout southern and Central Europe, North Africa and much of Asia, including Sri Lanka and Taiwan. In the British Isles it has been hunted to extinction, but it has been introduced from Europe into the USA, Hawaii and New Zealand. It is a natural inhabitant of deciduous woods and forests where it lives in groups of up to 20, though old males are solitary. It feeds on a wide range of foodstuffs, including tubers, bulbs, nuts and acorns, which it roots up with its tough, sensitive, mobile snout. It has a passion for the subterranean fungi known as truffles and it also eats insects and their larvae, small rodents, fish and, occasionally, carrion. It is a nocturnal and swift animal that is widely hunted for sport and for its flesh, of which the young boar's is considered a delicacy. Within its vast range the breeding season varies, but in Europe a litter of 4–10 longitudinally striped young is produced in March–April. Sometimes a second litter is produced the same year. Wild Boars grow to a length of 1.8m (5.9ft) with a 30cm (11.8in) tail. They are a richly symbolic animal (see also Domestic Pig) often associated with the protection of soldiers.

♂♀ Wolf *Canis lupus*

The fear that the Wolf once engendered in our ancestors is now only present as an atavistic trace in folk tales such as 'Little Red Riding Hood' and 'The Three Little Pigs', but in earlier times this intelligent and resourceful member of the dog family (Canidae) must have posed a real threat as a serious competitor for food. Even today we talk of 'keeping the wolf from the door' when contemplating hard times. The Wolf is the ancestor of the domestic dog. Once it was probably one of the most widespread mammals, but due to persecution and loss of habitat today it is only found in the wilder parts of Eurasia and North America. It inhabits the tundra, steppes and forests in packs comprising 1 or

several families. These are rarely larger than 10 individuals and they hunt co-operatively for moose, elk and reindeer (caribou), but the bulk of their diet consists of smaller prey, such as hares, birds, rodents, fish and carrion. They can lope along tirelessly for extended periods at speeds of 35–38km/h (roughly 22–24mph). Wolves mate for life and a litter of 3–8 young is born every year. Males are larger than females and northern populations bigger than southern ones and their size ranges between 1–1.4m (3.3–4.6ft) long with 30–48cm (11.8–18.9in) tails. Wolves have a prominent place in myth and legend and Romulus, the founder of Rome, and his twin brother Remus were said to have been raised by a she-wolf. Beowulf and other ancient Anglo-Saxon heroes and kings incorporated the name of the wolf into their own in the belief that the qualities of courage and endurance of this beast would become attached to them.

♂♀ Wolverine or Glutton *Gulo gulo*

The solitary Wolverine hunts a territory that may be as large as 1000 square km (621 square miles) for a wide range of food, which includes some plant matter such as berries but mainly rodents, birds and their eggs, insects, carrion and larger animals up to the size of deer and reindeer. It is thought that mostly old or sickly individuals of the latter are taken. It also raids traps and, given the chance, it will break into isolated human dwellings and steal what food it finds there. It has a strong disagreeable musky odour and is sometimes called a 'Skunk Bear'. The name 'Glutton' refers to the way it gorges itself. Wolverines are hunted for their fur that does not freeze when wet and makes an ideal lining for hoods and anoraks. They are largely terrestrial and distributed in the taiga and tundra of North America and Europe. Wolverines are the largest and most powerful species of mustelid and the larger males grow to a maximum length of 1.1m (3.6ft) with 26cm (10.2in) tails. Wolverines mate in the summer but due to delayed implantation the litter of 2–3 young is not born until the following spring – the ideal time for its survival.

♂♀ Wombat *Vombatus ursinus*

Wombats are shy, nocturnal marsupials that are native to the forested hills of the south-eastern seaboard of Australia and Tasmania. They live in burrows, about 2m (6.6ft) deep and up to 30m (98.4ft) long, at the end of which are grass-lined nests. Their principal food is grass, roots, tubers and fungi and they

can be a pest in some areas where they raid cornfields, with their burrowing activities often destroying fences in the process. They are frequently persecuted and also considered unwelcome because their abandoned burrows are likely to become homes to rabbits – a major Australian pest – and for the hazard these holes represent to horses and their riders. From May–July the female gives birth to a single young that stays in her rear-facing pouch for about 3 months. It eventually grows to an adult size of 0.9–1.2m (nearly 3–3.9ft).

♂♀ Yak *Bos mutus*

The Yak has been domesticated for 3000 years in Tibet where it is a valuable pack animal that also provides meat, leather and milk, which has a high fat content and is very nutritious. Its wool is woven into ropes and cloth and its dung provides the only available fuel in its treeless homeland. The wild Yak, however, is listed as an endangered species. The wild males are very much larger than the domesticated ones and attain a length of 3.2m (10.5ft) and a weight of up to 1 tonne (2205lb). The Yak's long coat protects it from the intense cold of winter on the steppes of the Tibetan Plateau where it lives at altitudes of up to 6100m (over 20,000ft). Female wild Yaks live in herds of 20–200 – sometimes up to 1000 – with their young and graze on grass, herbage and lichen while the males live in small bachelor herds or are solitary; they come together only in the winter mating season. A single young is born and both sexes eventually grow horns, which can be 1m (3.3ft) long in a mature male.

♂♀ Yapok or Water Opossum *Chironectes minimus*

The Yapok is found near freshwater lakes and streams from tropical Mexico throughout Central and South America as far south as Argentina at altitudes of up to 2000m (6562ft). It is the only marsupial to have adapted to an aquatic life and is solely carnivorous, preying on fish, crustaceans, amphibians and other small aquatic invertebrates and its presence in an area is often betrayed by piles of such remains. Yapoks are nocturnal and spend the days asleep in riverbank burrows and are nowadays scarce throughout their range. They mate in December and a litter of about 5 young is born as semi-embryos that continue to develop in their mother's pouch, which she is able to seal hermetically with a strong muscle when underwater. Yapoks are 27–40cm (10.6–15.8in) long with 31–43cm (12.2–16.9in) tails.

CONTEST RULES

To enter, complete the Official Entry Form on the fold-[...] portion of this page by hand printing the following [info]rmation: your name, your complete address, your [day]time telephone number, your date of birth, and the [ide]ntity and sex of the missing creature. Also, in thirty [wo]rds or less, provide a statement on why you believe that [the] Earth is the ultimate Noah's ark. Sign the official entry [for]m on the designated line. If appropriate, have parent or [gu]ardian also sign on the designated line. Entries must be [su]bmitted on an original Official Entry Form from the back [of] a copy of *The Ultimate Noah's Ark*. No facsimiles or [re]productions will be accepted.

[2.] Mail your completed entry to: The Ultimate Noah's Ark [C]ontest, Box 1532, Fairport, NY 14550. All entries must be [re]ceived by February 1, 1995. Proof of mailing is not [a]ccepted as proof of delivery. You may enter the contest a [m]aximum of five times; however, each entry must be on an [o]riginal Official Entry Form and each entry must be mailed [s]eparately. Sponsors will not be responsible for lost, [d]amaged, incomplete, illegible, or late mail.

[3]. Entries will be judged under the supervision of Power Group, Inc., an independent judging company whose decisions are final. The correct identification of the missing creature will earn 150 points, and the correct sex of the missing creature will earn 50 points. Your statement on why the Earth is the ultimate Noah's ark will be scored based on the following: appropriateness to theme (0-50), originality (0-10), clarity of expression (0-10), neatness (0-10). Prizes will be awarded in descending order (Grand, First, Runner-up) to the contestants with the highest point totals, i.e. the contestant with the highest score will win the Grand Prize; the contestants with the next ten highest scores will each win First Prize, etc. In the unlikely event of a tie at the Grand Prize level, the prize will be divided equally. If there are ties for First Prize or Runner-up, duplicate prizes will be awarded.

4. Prizes/values: Grand Prize (1) $10,000 cash; First Prize (10)

a limited-edition signed lithograph of the author's painting of the missing creature/$1,000; Runner up Prizes (50) a copy of *Pioneer Naturalists*/$22.50. Total prize value $21,125.

5. This competition is open to residents of the United States and Canada, except employees and families of the author, the publishers, their affiliates, the independent judging organization, and any other person or company involved with the administration of this program. Entrants under 18 years of age must have their entries signed by a parent or legal guardian. Entries submitted by a group must be identified by only one name and address. Any prize won will be awarded only to the person named. Void in Vermont and wherever else prohibited or restricted. All national, state, provincial, and local laws apply. Taxes on prizes are the winners' responsibility. Winners agree to allow their names and photographs to be used for advertising and publicity without additional compensation. There will be no substitution for the prizes offered.

6. All entries will become the property of the sponsors and will not be returned. Submission of an entry will be deemed to be acceptance of the rules by the entrant. Neither the author nor the publishers nor the judges will enter into correspondence regarding this competition. The sponsors reserve all rights in connection with this competition and in respect to any matter arising from it.

7. Canadian residents, in order to win, must first correctly answer a skill-testing question administered by mail. Any litigation regarding the conduct and awarding of a prize in this publicity contest by a resident of the Province of Quebec may be submitted to the Regis des loteries et courses du Quebec.

8. For a list of winners send a self-addressed stamped envelope to: The Ultimate Noah's Ark Winners, Box 1532, Fairport, NY 14550 between March 1, 1995, and May 31st, 1995.

OFFICIAL ENTRY FORM

Print all information clearly in block letters

Name ....

Address ....

....

Daytime Telephone Number ....

Signature ....

Date of Birth ....

Signature of parent or
guardian if entrant is under 18 ....

Identity of the Missing Creature ....

Sex of Missing Creature ....

In 30 words or less, tell us why you believe the Earth is the ultimate Noah's ark. (Please print in block letters.)

....

....

....

....

....

....

Mail Official Entry Form to:
The Ultimate Noah's Ark Contest
Box 1532
Fairport, NY 14550

Entries must be received by the judges by February 1, 1995.

Win $10,000 in THE ULTIMATE NOAH'S ARK Contest!

This is the start of a wonderful adventure. Take a grand tour through the animal kingdom and find depicted in various ways 707 creatures — 353 pairs and one without a match. The deceptively simple challenge is to find and name this solitary creature, which is among those listed in the accompanying text. In order to identify the missing creature, it will be necessary to find and name all the other animals in the painting. In his introduction, Mike Wilks makes some suggestions which may help you in this quest. The text also contains a number of clues, and male and female symbols have been included for you to check off the animals as you find them. When you think you have solved the mystery, complete the Official Entry Form, including a statement in 30 words or less on why you believe the Earth is the ultimate Noah's ark. The complete rules of the contest can be found on the reverse of this page.

THE PRIZES

The Grand Prize winner will receive $10,000!

10 First Prize winners will each receive an exclusive signed limited-edition lithograph of Mike Wilks's painting of the missing creature.

50 Runner-up Prize winners will each receive a copy of *Pioneer Naturalists*, by renowned nature writer Howard Ensign Evans.

Only Official Entry Forms will be accepted

Mail your entry to: The Ultimate Noah's Ark Contest
Box 1532
Fairport, NY 14550

Entries must be received by February 1, 1995.

See the reverse side for Official Entry Form and complete rules.